WORKING OUT

with Phonological Awareness

Linda R. Schreiber • Angela Sterling-Orth
Sarah A. Thurs • Nancy L. McKinley

Super Duper® Publications
Greenville, SC

© 2007 Super Duper® Publications
© 2000 by Thinking Publications

Permission is granted for the user to reproduce the material contained herein in limited form for classroom use only. Reproduction of this material for an entire school or school system is strictly prohibited. No part of this material may be reproduced (except as noted above), stored in a retrieval system, or transmitted in any form or by any means (mechanically, electronically, recording, web, etc.) without the prior written consent and approval of Super Duper® Publications.

10   09   08   07   06   05   9   8   7   6   5   4

Library of Congress Cataloging-in-Publication Data

Working out with phonological awareness / Linda R. Schreiber ... [et al.].
    p. cm.
  Includes bibliographical references.
  ISBN 1-888222-56-5 (pbk.)
    1. Phonetics—study and teaching (Elementary)—Handbooks, manuals, etc. 2. Language awareness in children—Handbooks, manuals, etc. I. Schreiber, Linda R. (Linda Rose), date.
  LB1573.3 .W67 2000
  372.46'5—dc21   00-057761

Printed in USA
Cover design by Debbie Olson

All brand names and product names used in this book are tradenames, servicemarks, trademarks, or registered trademarks of their respective owners.

www.superduperinc.com
1-800-277-8737

Acknowledgments

Special thanks to our reviewers—Denise Simmons, Monica Lapin, and Peggy Northrup and the elementary staff at Osseo Elementary School—for taking the time to field-test *Working Out with Phonological Awareness* and providing us with suggestions. Educators will appreciate the difference your comments made in improving this book.

We would also like to thank Heather Johnson and Stephanie Hora, for their technical-editing assistance, and Debbie Olson, for her wonderfully fun back cover design.

Contents

Introduction
    Overview 1
        Target Users 2
        Goals 3
    Phonological Awareness 3
        Definition 3
        Rationale 4
        Development 6
    Using *Working Out with Phonological Awareness* 8
        Uses 8
            Reinforcement and Review 8
            Informal Assessment 9
        When to Use 10
        Presenting the Exercises 10
        Exercise Directions 12
        Mediation of the Exercises 15
        Additional Suggestions 16

Appendix: Recording Form 20

References 23

Item Analysis 29

Workouts 35

v

Introduction

Overview

Working Out with Phonological Awareness has 50 quick, fun, pick-and-choose Workouts that provide phonological awareness practice. They are usable by educators and parents who want to provide extra practice in phonological awareness. The exercises review or reinforce skills that are emerging naturally or those that are being taught with a more comprehensive phonological awareness program (e.g., *Sounds Good to Me,* Bryant, 1998). The Workouts can be used as warm-ups prior to presentation of a more complete lesson, as cool-downs at the end of a lesson, or as quick exercises when a few extra minutes are available between activities at school or at home. The exercises can also be used informally to probe strengths and weaknesses in phonological awareness.

The skills targeted in the Workouts are appropriate for children 5 to 10 years old (kindergarten to fourth grade), but are also appropriate for older students who are lacking basic phonological awareness skills. Children do not need to be readers to complete the exercises, because they are simply asked to listen for, identify, blend, or manipulate *phonemes* (i.e., sounds), not to identify or respond with *letter* or *grapheme names.*

Each of the 50 Workouts includes six exercises focusing on the following phonological awareness skills:

1. Syllable segmentation

2. Rhyming

Working Out
with Phonological Awareness

3. Syllable and phoneme blending

4. Phoneme segmentation

5. Phoneme manipulation

6. Blending, segmenting, and manipulating phonemes in clusters

Each Workout also contains a Think About Challenge. These invite children to create their own exercise based on the six phonological awareness skills listed above.

As listed above, and as presented within each Workout, the phonological awareness skills are in order of development (e.g., syllable segmentation skills emerge before rhyming skills). An Item Analysis (see pages 29–34) provides a breakdown of the kinds and locations of the exercises (excluding the Think About Challenges). An exercise can be selected based on the type of skill, the level of difficulty, or both. Not all exercises within a Workout need to be completed; for example, exercises for a particular skill, such as rhyming, could be chosen from each of the 50 Workouts.

Target Users

The exercises in *Working Out with Phonological Awareness* are intended for use with children ages 5 to 10. All children who are prereaders or who are learning to read can benefit from the practice these exercises provide. In addition, the tasks are useful for children who have shown difficulty learning to read and write and for children who have expressive phonological disorders. The Workouts can be used by elementary teachers, speech-language pathologists, learning disabilities specialists, reading specialists, special educators, and families.

Goals

The main goal of *Working Out with Phonological Awareness* is to provide children with practice opportunities for improving their phonological awareness skills. In addition, exercises can be selected to use informally to determine a child's strengths and weaknesses in the area of phonological awareness. The following skills can be reinforced using the Workouts:

- Syllable segmentation of two-, three-, four-, and five-syllable words or word combinations and four- to eight-syllable sentences

- Rhyming

- Blending of two, three, four, and five syllables and blending of three, four, and five phonemes

- Sound segmentation in words with two, three, four, and five phonemes

- Sound manipulation, including deleting, adding, and substituting phonemes

- Blending, segmenting, and manipulating phonemes in clusters

Phonological Awareness

Definition

Phonological awareness—also referred to as *sound awareness*—is an awareness of "the ways in which words and syllables can be divided into smaller units" (Goswami and Bryant, 1990, p. 2). Goswami and Bryant describe three units of sounds within words: syllables; intra-syllabic units (i.e., larger than phonemes, but smaller than syllables), referred to as *onset* and *rime*; and phonemes (i.e., the smallest meaningful units of sound). For example, the word *fishing* can be broken down like this:

1. By syllables: *fish • ing*
2. By intra-syllabic units: *f-* (onset) and *-ishing* (rime)
3. By phonemes: /f/ /ɪ/ /ʃ/ /ɪ/ /~/

The most difficult of these units is the phoneme level, and thus *phonemic awareness* is the latest awareness to develop (Sawyer, 1987). Phonemic awareness is required for learning sound-symbol correspondence (van Kleeck, Gillam, and McFadden, 1998), that is, that words are comprised of letters that correspond to sounds. Phonemic awareness refers specifically to awareness of phonemes in words as is required for sound segmentation, sound manipulation, and sound blending (Hodson, 1994).

Phonological awareness, however, includes broader tasks such as rhyming, segmenting words into syllables, segmenting words into sounds, manipulating sounds, and blending sounds and syllables (Stackhouse, 1997). A primary goal of phonological awareness activities is to improve phonemic awareness, which in turn improves word recognition and spelling and, ultimately, reading comprehension and writing fluency.

Rationale

Phonological awareness is an important consideration for children because it is a strong predictor of literacy success (Adams, 1990; Blachman, 1994, 1997; Bradley and Bryant, 1983; Bryant, Bradley, MacLean, and Crossland, 1989; Cunningham, 1988; Lundberg, Frost, and Peterson, 1988; Kamhi and Catts, 1991; McBride-Chang, 1995). In particular, rhyming ability has been shown to predict early reading skills

(Bradley and Bryant, 1985). Swank and Catts (1994) have shown that strong readers are good at phonological awareness tasks and that poor readers have difficulty with phonological awareness tasks. Some researchers even consider deficiency in phonological awareness as the cause of some children's reading difficulties (Catts and Kamhi, 1999). Both reading and spelling require phonological awareness; reading especially requires blending skills and spelling especially requires segmentation skills (Ehri, 2000).

There is strong evidence that (1) phonological awareness skills can be improved through exercises and activities targeted at enhancing such skills (Adams, 1990; Blachman, 1989, 1994; Calfee, 1977; Torgesen, Wagner, and Rashotte, 1994); (2) phonological awareness can be effectively developed in prereaders to later have a positive effect on their literacy skills (Blachman, 1994; Lundberg et al., 1988; O'Connor, Jenkins, Leicester, and Slocum 1993; Warrick, Rubin, and Rowe-Walsh, 1993); and (3) improvement in phonological awareness has a positive impact on learning to read and write (Bradley and Bryant, 1985; Cunningham, 1988; Gillon and Dodd, 1995; Lundberg et al., 1988; O'Connor et al., 1993).

Phonological awareness is also important for children with speech and language disorders. Children with language disorders, especially those with phonological disorders, experience difficulty with phonological awareness tasks (Catts, 1993; Catts, Swank, McIntosh, and Stewart, 1989; Larrivee and Catts, 1999; Leitao, Hogben, and Fletcher, 1997; Stackhouse and Snowling, 1992).

Hodson (2000) and Fey, Catts, and Larrivee (1995) suggest developing phonological awareness skills in children with speech and language disorders as early as possible. Van Kleeck et al.'s (1998) research indicated positive outcomes of phonological awareness training with 4- and 5-year-old children who had speech and/or language disorders. Gillon (2000) explored the efficacy of phonological awareness intervention on reading performance and speech production for children identified as having expressive speech and language disorders and early reading delay. She found that children who received phonological awareness intervention made significantly more gains in phonological awareness ability, reading development, and speech articulation than children who had received other types of speech and language intervention. The children in her study even reached levels of reading performance similar to children with typically developing skills. Her findings therefore suggest that phonological awareness intervention not only improves phonological awareness ability, but it also has a positive impact on reading and speech production.

Development

Most children develop phonological awareness incidentally from everyday life (Stackhouse, 1997). Preschoolers are typically able to rhyme and segment by syllable (Liberman, Shankweiler, Fischer, and Carter, 1974). Preschool children tend to spontaneously rhyme; rhyming helps sensitize children to the sound structure in words (Dowker, 1989). These two early developing phonological awareness skills—rhyming and syllable segmentation—lay the foundation for later developing phonological awareness skills: blending, sound segmentation, and manipulation (Bryant et al., 1989; Liberman et al., 1974; MacLean, Bryant, and Bradley, 1987).

Introduction

The sequence of development delineated by Stackhouse (1997) appears to be the following: syllable segmentation, rhyming, syllable blending, phoneme blending, phoneme segmentation, sound manipulation, and cluster segmentation. This sequence is further supported by the following information:

1. It is easier for children to segment (e.g., tap out) syllables of words (usually developed by age 5) than to segment phonemes (usually developed by age 6) (Liberman et al., 1974).

2. Children can detect rhyme long before they can read (Bradley and Bryant, 1983, 1985). At first, children know that two words rhyme but do not know exactly which sound(s) the two words share (Goswami and Bryant, 1990). Judging whether words rhyme and matching rhyming words are both easier tasks than completing "oddity tasks," which ask "Which of these words does not rhyme with the others?" or supplying a word that rhymes with another (Hodson, 2000).

3. Phoneme blending is easier than phoneme segmentation (Harbers, 1999).

4. Children can identify the initial sounds in words before they can read (Stackhouse, 1997). Children are first able to detect and/or delete the beginning, single phoneme of a word (Goswami and Bryant, 1990), then they are able to detect and/or delete an ending phoneme, and then they are able to identify a sound in the medial position (Hubbard and Mahanna-Boden, 2000). Phoneme deletion from clusters or middles of words continues to cause children difficulty until 9 to 10 years of age (Bruce, 1964).

5. Phoneme deletion and manipulation of continuant sounds (e.g., *s, m*) are easier than deletion of noncontinuant sounds (e.g., stops *b, p, t, k*) (Content, Morais, Alegria, and Bertelson, 1982; Hubbard and Mahanna-Boden, 2000; Treiman and Baron, 1981).

Working Out with Phonological Awareness capitalizes on this developmental information by presenting its phonological awareness exercises hierarchically within each Workout. Users may pick and choose the most developmentally appropriate exercises within each Workout.

Using *Working Out with Phonological Awareness*

Uses

Working Out with Phonological Awareness can be used to reinforce and review or to informally assess phonological awareness skills. Each Workout contains one exercise for each of six types of phonological awareness skills and one Think About Challenge. Workouts can be used in their entirety or in part, depending on the skill level of the children involved.

Reinforcement and Review

The Workouts can be used to reinforce and review skills taught in a complete phonological awareness program, such as *Sounds Good to Me* (Bryant, 1998) or taught in other phonological awareness resources, such as *Silly Sounds Playground* (McKinley, Schreiber, Sterling-Orth, and Tobalsky, 1999). When using a Workout to reinforce or review phonological awareness skills, be sure to consider the relative ease or difficulty of each task. Since each Workout contains one exercise for each of the six phonological awareness skills and a Think About Challenge, a range of difficulty exists for each Workout. (Refer to the Item Analysis [see pages 29–34] for a detailed breakdown of the types and locations of exercises found in each Workout.)

This format allows you to address individual children's needs by picking and choosing appropriate exercises within a single Workout (e.g., doing only the Segmenting Syllables and Rhyming exercises when working with a kindergarten class, or choosing easy or difficult exercises from one Workout to match the skill level of each child in a group). If, however, you decide to present a Workout in its entirety, only expect responses for those tasks that are considered developmentally appropriate for the child.

Informal Assessment

The Workouts are also excellent stimuli for gathering data regarding a child's strengths and weaknesses in their phonological awareness development. Since a wide range of tasks are included, and they are arranged in hierarchical order, they can be used to probe a variety of skills.

Periodically, gather assessment data in a one-to-one situation with a child by presenting one or more appropriate exercises to him or her. Ideally, establish a baseline and measure change at key points—such as midyear, year-end, and/or during a review of an individualized education program (IEP). Use the *Recording Form* in the appendix (see pages 20–21) to indicate the child's correct and incorrect responses for each type of phonological awareness skill. This form can be used to collect data on up to 25 children. Duplicate additional copies as needed.

WORKING OUT
with Phonological Awareness

When to Use

Working Out with Phonological Awareness can be used at various times. A Workout can quickly be used at the beginning of a class or session to prepare students for learning. A complete Workout might be appropriate for a group of third graders; whereas a partial Workout might be all that is needed for a kindergarten group.

A Workout could also be used, in whole or in part, at the end of a lesson. This is especially helpful when a lesson has ended and there is insufficient time remaining to start a new lesson.

Consider using a Workout as a fun filler activity when a group of students is waiting for an event (e.g., before lunch, on bus rides, or while waiting for another activity to begin). The Workouts could also be offered as an option during "free time" or indoor recess, as long as an adult is available to read the exercises to the children.

Finally, exercises from a Workout could be used in a game-show fashion. Present an item to the entire group. The first child to raise his or her hand and respond accurately "wins" a sought-after privilege (e.g., being first in line or passing back papers).

Presenting the Exercises

When presenting an exercise, read each item aloud. With the exception of exercises that substitute vowel sounds (where long and short symbols were deemed necessary for correct pronunciation), pronunciation codings (e.g., using the International Phonetic Alphabet or dictionary pronunciation symbols) have been purposefully avoided to keep this

Introduction

resource reader-friendly. It is important to correctly pronounce the syllables and sounds. For example, when reading the syllable items, pronounce the italicized word parts (syllables) like they sound in the word they compose. Or when reading a single, italicized letter (or in the case of clusters, two or three letters), **pronounce the letter (or cluster) by the sound it makes,** rather than saying its letter or grapheme name(s) (e.g., say /k/ rather than *kay*). Also, be certain not to add a vowel sound when pronouncing consonant sounds (e.g., say /k/ rather than *kuh* and /st/ rather than *stuh*). Likewise, have children answer with a sound rather than a letter name when responding to the items in an exercise.

> Since the focus of this resource is on hearing sounds (not naming letters), a reminder to use sounds and not letter names appears in a gray box at the beginning of each Workout.

Be sure to provide explicit instructions for responding to each exercise, especially if an exercise type is new to a child or group of children. For example, when using a sound blending exercise for the first time, say something like "Listen to the sounds that I say. I want you to blend the sounds together so that they make a word. Here is a practice one: c • a • t. When I blend the sounds c • a • t together, it says *cat*." Provide additional examples whenever necessary. Explicit instructions are necessary because many of the exercises are contrived (i.e., they are not typical ways that children use words and sounds). Always be certain that the instructions are clear.

Care has been taken to control the vocabulary level of items in each exercise. However, for segmenting and blending

Working Out
with Phonological Awareness

words with four and five syllables, by nature of their length, they tend to be higher level. If necessary, substitute more appropriate terms or skip items that may be too challenging.

The answers to most exercises may be obvious. However, as a convenience, answers are provided in parentheses or in bold print for those items that might require thinking time.

Exercise Directions

As mentioned earlier, there are six exercises and one Think About Challenge per Workout. The following is a detailed description of each type of exercise with specific instructions when helpful.

1. *Segmenting Syllables:* Children practice segmenting syllables by recognizing or saying the parts of three-, four-, and five-syllable words or word combinations and four- to eight-syllable sentences. Tasks such as "Tap out the parts (syllables) in the word *uniform*," "Are there 2 or 3 parts (syllables) in the word *umbrella?*", and "Tell the number of parts (syllables) in the word *capital*" target recognition of syllables. Tasks like "Say *hot dog*. Now say *hot dog* without *dog*" and "Give a word that has four parts (syllables)" focus on generating the syllable segments.

    Note that the word *part* is used interchangeably with the term *syllable*. Choose the term that is appropriate for the level of the child you are using the exercises with.

2. *Rhyming:* Both rhyme recognition and generation are targeted with tasks such as "Give a word that rhymes with *chair*" and "Which word does not rhyme? *Block, dock, truck.*"

Introduction

Note that identifying a word that is different from the rest—oddity—is more difficult than naming a word that is the same. Also note that in rhyming items, it is permissible for children to respond with nonsense words, since the goal of the exercise is to hear the rime.

3. *Blending Syllables/Sounds:* Each Workout contains either a syllable or a sound blending task. Children blend two, three, or four syllables (e.g., "Does *to • ma • to* say *tomato* or *tornado?*" and "Blend these parts (syllables) together. What word do they make? *rea • der*") and blend three, four, or five sounds to form a word (e.g., "Does *b • a • b • y* say *maybe?*" and "Blend these sounds together. What word do they make? *l • i • ne*").

Be certain to pause slightly (e.g., for a second) at each bullet point in order to fully segment the word. Also be sure to pronounce each syllable or sound like it would sound in the word from which it is segmented.

4. *Segmenting Sounds in Words:* Children segment sounds through a variety of recognition tasks (e.g., "How many sounds do you hear in the word *wish?*", "Do these words end with the same sound? *crash, push*," "Does this word have 3 sounds? *popcorn*," and "Does this word begin with a *f* sound? *fender*") and generation tasks (e.g., "Think of a word that ends with *t*," "Think of a word that begins with the same sound as *six*," and "What sounds do you hear in this word? *bug*").

Remember to pronounce single, italicized letters by the sounds they make, rather than their letter or grapheme names.

Working Out
with Phonological Awareness

5. *Manipulating Sounds:* Children delete a sound (e.g., "Say *page*. Now say *page* without the ending sound"); add a sound (e.g., "Say *free*. Now add a *z* sound to the end of *free*"); determine which sound was deleted or added (e.g., "Say *trees,* then say *tree*. What sound makes these two words different?"); or substitute a sound (e.g., "Say *hug*. Now say *hug* with a *t* sound instead of the *g* sound").

    Remember to pronounce single, italicized letters by the sounds they make, rather than their letter or grapheme names.

    Occasionally in sound manipulation exercises, nonsense words are used in the items. This is purposeful, since true understanding of phoneme manipulation would seem to mean that children can also apply the skill to nonsense words. Similarly, some responses will also be nonsense words.

6. *Working with Clusters:* Manipulation of consonant sounds within blends is included to give children practice at the most difficult level of sound manipulation. Children blend the sounds in words containing consonant clusters (e.g., "Blend these sounds together. What word do they make? *c • l • a • ss*"); segment words that contain consonant clusters (e.g., "How many sounds do you hear in the word *blue?*", "What are the sounds in the word *cloak?*", and "Does this word end with *mp? lamp*"). They also generate words with clusters (e.g., "Think of a word that begins with *gr*" and "Think of a word that begins with the same two sounds as *drink*").

14

Introduction

Remember to pronounce the clustered italicized letters (e.g., *st*) by the sounds they make, rather than by their letter or grapheme names. Also for items requiring blending, remember to pause for a second at the bullet points.

7. *Think About Challenge:* Each Workout contains a Think About Challenge that asks children to use a variety of phonological awareness skills to complete a task. The items are considered challenging because they encourage thinking and are meant to extend children's phonological awareness. Frequently, children are asked to create their own task similar to ones they have already completed.

Mediation of the Exercises

As structured, the Workout exercises provide an abundance of practice for phonological awareness. Adults using the material should be aware that children may fail to apply the skills used in the Workout exercises to other relevant activities unless mediation accompanies the exercises.

When an adult mediates for a child, he or she focuses the child's attention on salient characteristics of the task with the intention to go beyond the task at hand. The concern is not just to have the child respond to the phonological awareness exercises, but to understand the skills and strategies needed to perform the exercise and to recognize when else those skills and strategies are required in academic, social, or vocational situations.

A prime way to focus a child's attention is to present questions such as the following:

- "Are you finding these exercises easy or hard? Why?"

Working Out
with Phonological Awareness

- "Now that we've done a few items, let's stop and think about how you're figuring out your answers. What do you do in your mind to find the answers?"

- "When have you used (name the skill: blending, segmenting, etc.) at school?"

Younger children will almost always need help verbalizing their responses. Be prepared to model a response using language at the child's level. Even older children frequently need help formulating their responses since often they can do the tasks but they cannot explain what they were thinking about or what makes certain activities challenging for them. Without assistance from an adult mediator, children may also fail to see how phonological awareness skills can help them in places other than the school setting.

Certainly you can use the exercises in this book in a straightforward manner without ever discussing them. However, mediated learning theory (Feuerstein, 1980) suggests that combining mediation with the exercises facilitates generalization of the skills. This helps the child be more receptive to learning about the same skills (in this case, phonological awareness skills) in other situations. It also helps children connect what they have learned to related skills; therefore, they become independent learners.

Additional Suggestions

1. As children take turns responding to items in the exercises, involve the children waiting for their turn in active listening. For example, have them give a thumbs-up or thumbs-down signal to indicate if a player accurately responds to an item.

Introduction

Another option is to randomly call on another child to listen to and repeat the responding child's guess if the responding child answers appropriately. This opportunity may improve motivation to listen during other players' turns.

Alternatively, use the Workouts as the basis for a competitive game between two teams. Award points or chips to teams for correct answers. Use the Think About Challenge exercises to break ties or to award bonus points. Be creative in how you set up the game rules, or involve students in deciding how to structure the game.

2. When a child is struggling to respond to an item, provide as much scaffolding and cuing as needed to help him or her succeed in the task. The following are examples:

   a. Repeat the text that contains the important information. For example, for the item that reads, "Say *sit*. Now say *sit* with a *p* sound instead of the *t* sound," repeat to the child, "Say *sit* with a *p* sound instead of the *t* sound" instead of rereading the entire item.

   b. Provide manipulatives that can support the child's performance. This could include tokens or small wooden blocks. For example, when asking a child to tell how many parts (syllables) are in a word, have him or her use small wooden blocks to represent and count the word parts or when asking a child to tell what sounds are in a word, use different colored blocks to represent each sound.

c. Provide visual and/or kinesthetic support for the child. For example, have the child watch your mouth and tell the beginning sound he or she hears in the word *boat*. Describe the manner and place of sound production (e.g., saying, "See how my lips pop open when I make the *p* sound at the end of the word *rope?*").

d. Have the child repeat slow, segmented productions of sounds or syllables following the model provided in the item. For example, when asking the child to tell how many parts (syllables) are in the word *capital*, have him or her repeat *cap • i • tal* several times while you model tapping out the number of syllables. Another alternative is to have the child show the number by raising his or her fingers as a visual cue upon hearing each sound or syllable.

e. Change the item to reflect a more dramatic contrast between the words. For example, if an item asks whether *light* and *line* rhyme, you may want to ask whether *light* and *bag*, or *line* and *hop*, rhyme.

f. Prolong continuant sounds (e.g., stridents *s, z*) while producing the model for the child (Lewkowicz, 1980). For example, when asking the child to say *soon* without the beginning sound, prolong the *s* sound.

g. Use repetition of noncontinuant sounds (e.g., stops *p, t, k*) while producing the item (Lewkowicz, 1980). For example, when asking the child to tell if the word *pickle* starts with a *p* sound, say "*p-p-p-pickle.*" (Do not use repetition if the child shows signs of being disfluent.)

Introduction

    h. Provide multiple choices for the child. For example, if an item asks the child to tell the number of parts (syllables) in the word *television,* ask the child if *television* has three, four, or five parts.

    i. If a child does not understand the term *rhyme,* for the rhyming exercises, provide three words that rhyme and have them generate a fourth word. For example, say, "*Cat, bat, hat*—what word could come next?"

    j. If a child experiences difficulty segmenting or blending sound sequences, substitute a consonant-vowel pattern (e.g., *bow),* which is easier than vowel-consonant patterns (e.g., *ice)* and consonant-vowel-consonant patterns (the most difficult) (e.g., *bug)* (Hubbard and Mahanna-Boden, 2000).

    k. Substitute jumping for clapping or tapping out the syllables of a word or sentence. Involving a larger motoric movement, such as jumping, can make the segmentation tasks more visible and therefore easier.

3. Children who struggle with the idea of blending sounds or syllables together can alternatively be told something like "I will say a word slowly." Then, you say it fast. Children who have difficulty segmenting words can be told to say the word slowly (e.g., *sssuuunnn).*

Appendix

WORKING OUT
with Phonological Awareness
Recording Form

Phonological Awareness Skill Areas

1. Syllable Segmentation	2. Rhyming	3. Syllable and Phoneme Blending	4. Phoneme Segmentation	5. Phoneme Manipulation	6. Cluster Manipulation	Comments

Names

Appendix

Names

References

Adams, M. (1990). *Beginning to read: Thinking and learning about print.* Cambridge, MA: MIT Press.

Blachman, B. (1989). Phonological awareness and word recognition: Assessment and intervention. In A. Kamhi and H. Catts (Eds.), *Reading disabilities: A developmental language perspective* (pp. 133–158). Boston: College Hill Press.

Blachman, B. (1994). Early literacy acquisition: The role of phonological awareness. In G. Wallach and K. Butler (Eds.), *Language learning disabilities in school-age children and adolescents* (pp. 253–274). New York: Macmillan.

Blachman, B. (Ed.). (1997). *Foundations of reading acquisition and dyslexia: Implications for early intervention.* Mahweh, NJ: Erlbaum.

Bradley, L., and Bryant, P.E. (1983). Categorizing sounds and learning to read: A causal connection. *Nature, 301,* 419–521.

Bradley, L., and Bryant, P.E. (1985). *Rhyme and reason in reading and spelling.* Ann Arbor: University of Michigan Press.

Bruce, D.J. (1964). The analysis of word sounds. *British Journal of Educational Psychology, 34,* 158–170.

Bryant, J. (1998). *Sounds good to me.* Eau Claire, WI: Thinking Publications.

Bryant, P.E., Bradley, L., MacLean, M., and Crossland, J. (1989). Nursery rhymes, phonological skills and reading. *Journal of Child Language, 16,* 407–428.

Calfee, R.C. (1977). Assessment of independent reading skills: Basic research and practical applications. In A.S. Reber and D.L. Scarborough (Eds.), *Toward a psychology of reading* (pp. 289–323). New York: Erlbaum.

Catts, H. (1993). The relationship between speech-language impairments and reading disabilities. *Journal of Speech and Hearing Research, 36,* 948–958.

Catts, H., and Kamhi, A. (1999). Causes of reading disabilities. In H. Catts and A. Kamhi (Eds.), *Language and reading disabilities* (pp. 95–127). Boston: Allyn and Bacon.

Catts, H., Swank, L., McIntosh, S., and Stewart, L. (1989, November). *Precursors of reading disabilities in language-impaired children.* Paper presented at the annual convention of the American Speech-Language-Hearing Association, St. Louis, MO.

Content, A., Morais, J., Alegria J., and Bertelson, P. (1982). Accelerating the development of phonetic segmentation skills in kindergartners. *Cahiers de Psychologie Cognitive, 2,* 259–269.

Cunningham, A.E. (1988, April). *A developmental study of instruction in phonemic awareness.* Paper presented at the annual meeting of the American Educational Research Association, New Orleans, LA.

Dowker, A. (1989). Rhyme and alliteration in poems elicited from young children. *Journal of Child Language, 16,* 181–202.

Ehri, L. (2000). Learning to read and learning to spell: Two sides of a coin. *Topics in Language Disorders, 20*(3), 19–36.

Feuerstein, R. (1980). *Instrumental enrichment.* Chicago: Scott Foresman.

Fey, M., Catts, H., and Larrivee, L. (1995). Preparing preschoolers for the academic and social challenges of school. In M. Fey, J. Windsor, and S. Warren (Eds.), *Language intervention: Preschool through the elementary years* (pp. 3–37). Baltimore: Brookes.

Gillon, G. (2000). The efficacy of phonological awareness intervention for children with spoken language impairment. *Language, Speech, and Hearing Services in Schools, 31,* 126–141.

References

Gillon, G., and Dodd, B. (1995). The effects of training phonological, semantic, and syntactic processing skills in spoken language on reading ability. *Language, Speech, and Hearing Services in Schools, 26,* 58–68.

Goswami, U., and Bryant, P.E. (1990). *Phonological skills and learning to read.* Hillsdale, NJ: Erlbaum.

Harbers, H. (1999, February). *Incorporating awareness in phonological intervention.* Presentation at the annual convention of the Illinois Speech-Language-Hearing Association, Arlington Heights, IL.

Hodson, B. (1994). Foreword. *Topics in Language Disorders, 14*(2), vi–viii.

Hodson, B. (2000, March). *Enhancing phonological and metaphonological skills: What we know in the year 2000.* Presentation at the annual convention of the Wisconsin Speech-Language-Hearing Association, Milwaukee, WI.

Hubbard, C., and Mahanna-Boden, S. (2000, February). *Phonological awareness: Assessment and training activities.* Presentation at the annual convention of the Kentucky Speech-Language-Hearing Association, Louisville, KY.

Kamhi, A., and Catts, A. (1991). *Reading disabilities: A developmental language perspective.* Boston: Allyn and Bacon.

Larrivee, L., and Catts, H. (1999). Early reading achievement in children with expressive phonological disorders. *American Journal of Speech-Language Pathology, 8*(2), 137–148.

Leitao, S., Hogben, J., and Fletcher, J. (1997). Phonological processing skills in speech and language impaired children. *European Journal of Disorders of Communication, 32,* 73–93.

Lewkowicz, N. (1980). Phonemic awareness training: What to teach and how to teach it. *Journal of Educational Psychology, 72,* 686–700.

Liberman, I.Y., Shankweiler, D., Fischer, F.W., and Carter, B. (1974). Reading and the awareness of linguistic segments. *Journal of Experimental Child Psychology, 18,* 201–212.

Lundberg, I., Frost, J., and Peterson, O.P. (1988). Effects of an extensive program for stimulating phonological awareness in preschool children. *Reading Research Quarterly, 23,* 263–284.

MacLean, M., Bryant, P.E., and Bradley, L. (1987). Rhymes, nursery rhymes and reading in early childhood. *Merrill-Palmer Quarterly, 33,* 255–281.

McBride-Chang, C. (1995). What is phonological awareness? *Journal of Educational Psychology, 87,* 179–192.

McKinley, N.L., Schreiber, L.R., Sterling-Orth, A., and Tobalsky, S.A. (1999). *Silly sounds playground.* Eau Claire, WI: Thinking Publications.

O'Connor, R.E., Jenkins, J.R., Leicester, N., and Slocum, T.A. (1993). Teaching phonological awareness to young children with learning disabilities. *Exceptional Children, 59*(6), 532–546.

Sawyer, D. (1987). *Test of awareness of language segments.* Austin, TX: Pro-Ed.

Stackhouse, J. (1997). Phonological awareness: Connecting speech and literacy problems. In B.W. Hodson and M.L. Edwards (Eds.), *Perspectives in applied phonology* (pp. 157–196). Gaithersburg, MD: Aspen.

Stackhouse, J., and Snowling, M. (1992). Barriers to literacy development in two cases of developmental verbal dyspraxia. *Cognitive Neuropsychology, 9,* 273–299.

Swank, L., and Catts, H. (1994). Phonological awareness and written word decoding. *Language, Speech, and Hearing Services in Schools, 25,* 9–14.

References

Torgesen, J.K., Wagner, R.K., and Rashotte, C.A. (1994). Longitudinal studies of phonological processing and reading. *Journal of Learning Disabilities, 27,* 776–786.

Treiman, R., and Baron, J. (1981). Segmental analysis ability: Development and relation to reading ability. In G. MacKinnon and T. Waller (Eds.), *Reading research: Advances in theory and practice* (Vol. 3, pp. 159–198). New York: Academic Press.

van Kleeck, A., Gillam, R., and McFadden, T. (1998). A study of classroom-based phonological awareness training for preschoolers with speech and/or language disorders. *American Journal of Speech-Language Pathology, 7*(3), 65–76.

Warrick, N., Rubin, H., and Rowe-Walsh, S. (1993). Phoneme awareness in language delayed children: Comparative studies and intervention. *Annals of Dyslexia, 43,* 153–173.

Item Analysis

Exercise Type	Workout Number

Segmenting Syllables

Recognition

Clap/Tap out the parts (syllables) in the word(s)	1, 4, 9, 15, 20, 21, 29, 33, 34, 39, 46, 50
Tell the number of parts (syllables) in the word	18, 23, 31, 37, 42, 44
Tell how many parts (syllables) are in the whole sentence	2, 10, 16, 22, 30, 45
Are there # or # parts (syllables) in the word X?	3, 11, 17, 36

Generation

Give a word/name that has # parts (syllables)	5, 6, 12, 24, 25, 28, 35, 41, 48
Say a sentence with # parts	7, 14, 26, 43, 49
Say X. Now say X without X	8, 13, 19, 27, 32, 38, 40, 47

Rhyming

Recognition

Do these two words rhyme?	1, 4, 11, 21, 23, 34, 41, 47

Code
= a number   X = a word
* = a sound

Working Out
with Phonological Awareness

Exercise Type	Workout Number
Which of these words rhymes with X: X, X, or X?	5, 8, 12, 24, 26, 35, 45, 48
Which word does not rhyme?	2, 7, 17, 20, 31, 42, 50

Generation

Give a word that rhymes with X	6, 9, 14, 16, 27, 29, 36, 44
Give 2 words that rhyme with X	15, 25, 28, 32, 37, 39, 43, 49
Give 3 words that rhyme with X	3, 13, 18, 19, 30, 40
Fill in the blank with a rhyming word	10, 22, 33, 38, 46

Blending Syllables

Recognition

For 3 Syllables	
Does * • * • * say X?	1
Does * • * • * say X or X?	3, 22, 23
For 4 Syllables	
Does * • * • * • * say X?	29
Does * • * • * • * say X or X?	6, 41, 46
For 5 Syllables	
Does * • * • * • * • * say X?	39
Does * • * • * • * • * say X or X?	14, 32, 36

Generation

Blend these parts (syllables) together. What word do they make?

For 2 syllables	10, 34, 50

Code
\# = a number   X = a word
* = a sound

30

Item Analysis

Exercise Type	Workout Number
For 3 syllables	5, 17, 26, 43
For 4 syllables	12, 20, 38
For 5 syllables	8, 27, 45

Blending Sounds

Recognition

For 3 Sounds	
Does * • * • * say X?	18
Does * • * • * say X or X?	2, 4, 21
For 4 Sounds	
Does * • * • * • * say X?	7
Does * • * • * • * say X or X?	11, 35, 44
For 5 Sounds	
Does * • * • * • * • * say X?	25
Does * • * • * • * • * say X or X?	9, 40, 48

Generation

Blend these sounds together. What word do they make?

For 3 sounds	13, 15, 33, 42
For 4 sounds	16, 28, 31, 37, 49
For 5 sounds	19, 24, 30, 47

Segmenting Sounds in Words

Recognition

How many sounds do you hear in the word?	1, 17, 28, 40

Code
\# = a number   X = a word
* = a sound

WORKING OUT
with Phonological Awareness

Exercise Type	Workout Number
Do these words begin with the same sound?	7, 19, 27, 38
Do these words end with the same sound?	2, 20, 30, 41
Does this word have # sounds?	8, 18, 29, 39
Does this word begin with a * sound?	12, 23, 31, 46
Does this word end with a * sound?	3, 21, 33, 42
Do you hear a * sound in this word?	9, 24, 32, 45

Generation

What sound does this word begin with, * or *?	4, 10, 35, 43
What sound does this word end with, * or *?	13, 49
Think of a word that begins with *	14, 22, 34, 44
Think of a word that ends with *	11, 25, 47
Think of a word that begins with the same sound as X	15, 26, 48
Think of a word that ends with the same sound as X	5, 36, 50
What sounds do you hear in this word?	6, 16, 37

Code
\# = a number   X = a word
* = a sound

Item Analysis

Exercise Type	Workout Number

Manipulating Sounds

Recognition

Say X, then say X. What sound makes these two words different?	12, 31, 34, 39
Say X, then say X. What sound was taken away from X to make X?	45, 49
Say X, then say X. What sound was added to X to make X?	6, 23

Generation

Say X. Now say X without the ending sound	2, 8, 14, 20, 26, 33, 37, 43
Say X. Now add a * sound to the end of X	5, 17, 27, 38, 44, 47
Say X. Now say X without the beginning sound	3, 9, 15, 21, 24, 29, 32, 35, 36, 40, 46
Say X. Now add a * sound to the beginning of X	1, 11, 16, 22, 30, 42
Say X. Now add a * sound to the end/beginning of X	7, 13, 19, 28, 50
Say X. Now say X with a * sound instead of a * sound	4, 10, 18, 25, 41, 48

Working with Clusters

Recognition—Segmenting a Cluster

How many sounds do you hear in the word?	1, 9, 20, 30
Does X have # sounds?	23, 36

Code
\# = a number   X = a word
* = a sound

Working Out
with Phonological Awareness

Exercise Type	Workout Number
Does this word begin with *?	3, 16, 28, 49
Does this word end with *?	10, 33, 40

Recognition—Manipulating a Cluster

Say X, then say X. What makes these two words different?	14, 17, 27

Generation—Blending a Cluster

Blend these sounds together. What word do they make?	6, 37, 48, 50

Generation—Segmenting a Cluster

What two sounds does this word begin with, ** or **?	4, 41, 45
What two sounds does this word end with, ** or **?	13, 25, 39
Think of a word that begins with *	2, 18, 34
Think of a word that begins with the same two sounds as X	5, 46
What are the sounds in the word?	12, 24, 31, 42

Generation—Manipulating a Cluster

Say X. Now say X without the * sound	7, 8, 26, 47
Say X. Now say X without the beginning sound	11, 35
Say X. Now say X with a * sound instead of the * sound	21, 32, 43
Say X. Now add a * sound to the end/beginning of X	15, 19, 22, 29, 38, 44

Code
= a number   X = a word
* = a sound

Workouts

Phonological Awareness
Workout #1

> ☞ When pronouncing an italicized letter (e.g., *t*), be sure to pronounce it by the sound it makes, rather than saying its letter name *(tee)* or adding a vowel to it *(ta)*.

Segmenting Syllables

Tap out the parts (syllables) in the word(s):

Saturday (3)   *refrigerator* (5)

cereal (3)   *centimeter* (4)

watermelon (4)   *pumpernickel bread* (5)

Rhyming

Do these two words rhyme?

splash, flash (Y)   *train, day* (N)

giggle, jiggle (Y)   *puddle, noodle* (N)

late, skate (Y)   *bobbing, bubble* (N)

Blending Syllables

Does *um • brell • a* say *umbrella?* (Y)

Does *mi • cro • scope* say *microphone?* (N)

Does *com • pu • ter* say *computer?* (Y)

Does *swimm • ing • pool* say *swimming pool?* (Y)

Does *spinn • ing • wheel* say *steering wheel?* (N)

Workout #1

Segmenting Sounds in Words

How many sounds do you hear in the word:

    shape (3)   *two* (2)   *tie* (2)

    wish (3)   *reading* (5)   *shiny* (4)

Manipulating Sounds

Say *age*. Now add a *p* sound to the beginning of *age*. *(page)*

Say *end*. Now add a *s* sound to the beginning of *end*. *(send)*

Say *ink*. Now add a *l* sound to the beginning of *ink*. *(link)*

Say *oak*. Now add a *j* sound to the beginning of *oak*. *(joke)*

Say *ice*. Now add a *m* sound to the beginning of *ice*. *(mice)*

Working with Clusters

How many sounds do you hear in the word:

    shrimp (5)   *blue* (3)   *cream* (4)

    stretch (5)   *crunch* (5)   *press* (4)

Think About Challenge

Think of a word with 3 parts (syllables) that begins with a *p* sound.

Phonological Awareness
Workout #2

☞ When pronouncing an italicized letter (e.g., *t*), be sure to pronounce it by the sound it makes, rather than saying its letter name *(tee)* or adding a vowel to it *(ta)*.

Segmenting Syllables

Tell how many parts (syllables) are in the whole sentence:
The refrigerator is new. (8)
Her name is Julie. (5)
She is sixteen. (4)
How many cookies are left? (7)
The dog is furry. (5)

Rhyming

Which word does not rhyme?

block, dock, **truck**
zipper, **glitter,** *flipper*
sneaker, speaker, **joker**

toy, foil, spoil
dress, **best,** *guess*
fish, dish, **leash**

Blending Sounds

Does *t* • *ow* • *n* say *down* or **town?**
Does *c* • *oa* • *t* say **coat** or *coach?*
Does *g* • *oo* • *se* say **goose** or *loose?*
Does *p* • *e* • *n* say **pen** or *pin?*
Does *h* • *ea* • *d* say **head** or *lead?*

Workout #2

Segmenting Sounds in Words

Do these words end with the same sound?

    crash, push (Y)   *north, south* (Y)   *thick, let* (N)

    cup, pin (N)   *tool, well* (Y)   *those, rise* (Y)

Manipulating Sounds

Say *whoosh*. Now say *whoosh* without the ending sound. *(whoo)*

Say *pouch*. Now say *pouch* without the ending sound. *(pow)*

Say *Ross*. Now say *Ross* without the ending sound. *(raw)*

Say *bait*. Now say *bait* without the ending sound. *(bay)*

Say *page*. Now say *page* without the ending sound. *(pay)*

Working with Clusters

Think of a word that begins with:

    fr   *sp*   *shr*

    pl   *gr*   *sl*

Think About Challenge

Think of a word with 2 parts (syllables) that rhymes with another word with 2 parts (syllables).

Phonological Awareness
Workout #3

> ☞ When pronouncing an italicized letter (e.g., *t*), be sure to pronounce it by the sound it makes, rather than saying its letter name *(tee)* or adding a vowel to it *(ta)*.

Segmenting Syllables

Are there 3 or 4 parts (syllables) in the word *February?* (4)

Are there 4 or 5 parts (syllables) in the word *Mississippi?* (4)

Are there 3 or 4 parts (syllables) in the word *museum?* (3)

Are there 2 or 3 parts (syllables) in the word *airplane?* (2)

Are there 3 or 4 parts (syllables) in the word *calendar?* (3)

Rhyming

Give 3 words that rhyme with:

bite	*blue*	*juice*
snap	*going*	*hand*

Blending Syllables

Does *con • fess • ion* say **confession** or *confusion?*

Does *o • ffic • ial* say *officer* or **official?**

Does *med • i • cine* say *Madison* or **medicine?**

Does *o • ver • shoot* say *overshot* or **overshoot?**

Does *to • ma • to* say **tomato** or *tornado?*

Workout #3

Segmenting Sounds in Words

Does this word end with with a *k* sound?

pack (Y) *tan* (N) *took* (Y)
could (N) *jug* (N) *gone* (N)

Manipulating Sounds

Say *tail*. Now say *tail* without the beginning sound. *(ail)*
Say *bite*. Now say *bite* without the beginning sound. *(ite)*
Say *tape*. Now say *tape* without the beginning sound. *(ape)*
Say *ripe*. Now say *ripe* without the beginning sound. *(ipe)*
Say *wall*. Now say *wall* without the beginning sound. *(all)*

Working with Clusters

Does this word begin with *st*?

stood (Y) *sting* (Y) *still* (Y)
past (N) *slippery* (N) *stick* (Y)

Think About Challenge

Think of a word that has 5 sounds.

Phonological Awareness
Workout #4

> ☞ When pronouncing an italicized letter (e.g., *t*), be sure to pronounce it by the sound it makes, rather than saying its letter name *(tee)* or adding a vowel to it *(ta)*.

Segmenting Syllables

Tap out the parts (syllables) in the word(s):

    Humpty Dumpty (4)   *supermarket* (4)

    uniform (3)   *permission* (3)

    neighborhood (3)   *magnifying glass* (5)

Rhyming

Do these two words rhyme?

    cat, hat (Y)   *big, kiss* (N)   *stream, street* (N)

    shelf, held (N)   *roof, poof* (Y)   *tags, takes* (N)

Blending Sounds

Does *e* • *gg* • *s* say **eggs** or LEGOs?

Does *ch* • *u* • *ck* say chalk or **chuck?**

Does *l* • *a* • *p* say lab or **lap?**

Does *w* • *i* • *fe* say **wife** or life?

Does *f* • *i* • *ll* say **fill** or file?

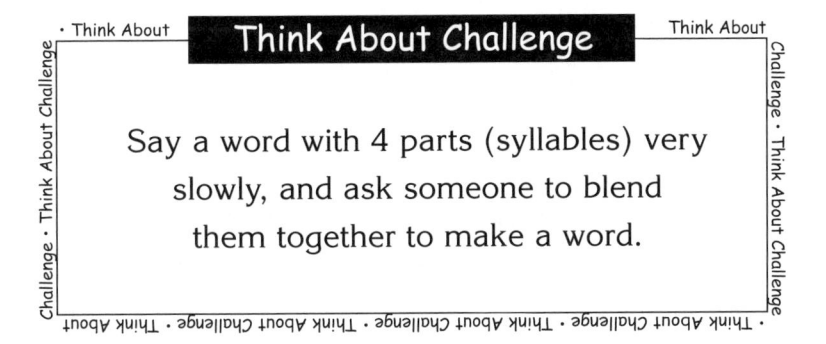

Workout #4

Segmenting Sounds in Words

What sound does this word begin with, *t* or *d?*

    *d*inner   *t*opic   *t*iger

    *d*oorway   *t*omorrow   *t*oast

Manipulating Sounds

Say *bead*. Now say *bead* with a *p* sound instead of the *d* sound.
    (beep)

Say *sit*. Now say *sit* with a *p* sound instead of the *t* sound. *(sip)*

Say *cat*. Now say *cat* with a *f* sound instead of the *t* sound. *(calf)*

Say *hat*. Now say *hat* with a *m* sound instead of the *t* sound. *(ham)*

Say *hug*. Now say *hug* with a *t* sound instead of the *g* sound. *(hut)*

Working with Clusters

What two sounds does this word begin with, *st* or *sk?*

    *st*and   *s*coot (sk)   *sk*ip

    *st*ick   *s*cum (sk)   *st*uck

Think About Challenge

Say a word with 4 parts (syllables) very slowly, and ask someone to blend them together to make a word.

Phonological Awareness
Workout #5

> ☞ When pronouncing an italicized letter (e.g., *t*), be sure to pronounce it by the sound it makes, rather than saying its letter name *(tee)* or adding a vowel to it *(ta)*.

Segmenting Syllables

Give a word that has:

    3 parts (syllables)

    4 parts (syllables)

    5 parts (syllables)

Rhyming

Which of these words rhymes with

    heart: heat, **smart,** or hear?

    phone: **stone,** comb, or moon?

    yellow: belly, **Jell-O,** or hill?

    jump: joke, **bump,** or drum?

    farm: dog, barn, or **arm?**

Blending Syllables

Blend these parts (syllables) together. What word do they make?

    e • ra • ser   con • sid • er   au • di • ence

    un • der • stand   a • llow • ance   ratt • le • snake

Workout #5

Segmenting Sounds in Words

Think of a word that ends with the same sound as:

    stiff   *water*   *tonight*

    that   *fish*   *sail*

Manipulating Sounds

Say *core*. Now add a *n* sound to the end of *core*. *(corn)*

Say *door*. Now add a *m* sound to the end of *door*. *(dorm)*

Say *sue*. Now add a *p* sound to the end of *sue*. *(soup)*

Say *due*. Now add a *k* sound to the end of *due*. *(duke)*

Say *fly*. Now add a *t* sound to the end of *fly*. *(flight)*

Working with Clusters

Think of a word that begins with the same two sounds as:

    stick   *fry*   *glass*

    drink   *please*   *sleep*

Think About Challenge

Think of a word with 3 parts (syllables) that ends with the same sound as *canopy*.

Phonological Awareness
Workout #6

> ☞ When pronouncing an italicized letter (e.g., *t*), be sure to pronounce it by the sound it makes, rather than saying its letter name *(tee)* or adding a vowel to it *(ta)*.

Segmenting Syllables

Give a person's name that has:

   3 parts (syllables)

   4 parts (syllables)

   5 parts (syllables)

Rhyming

Give a word that rhymes with:

tip	*wing*	*bed*
bug	*chair*	*car*

Blending Syllables

Does *ded • i • ca • tion* say **dedication** or *definition?*

Does *in • stru • men • tal* say **instrumental** or *elemental?*

Does *di • strib • u • tor* say *contributor* or **distributor?**

Does *hu • mid • i • ty* say *humility* or **humidity?**

Does *se • cur • i • ty* say **security** or *impurity?*

Segmenting Sounds in Words

What sounds do you hear in this word?

take   *when*   *gooey*

picking   *muffin*   *bug*

Manipulating Sounds

Say *pay*, then say *pain*. What sound was added to *pay* to make *pain*? *(n)*

Say *car*, then say *cars*. What sound was added to *car* to make *cars*? *(z)*

Say *Ed*, then say *head*. What sound was added to *Ed* to make *head*? *(h)*

Say *pie*, then say *pipe*. What sound was added to *pie* to make *pipe*? *(p)*

Say *in*, then say *chin*. What sound was added to *in* to make *chin*? *(ch)*

Working with Clusters

Blend these sounds together. What word do they make?

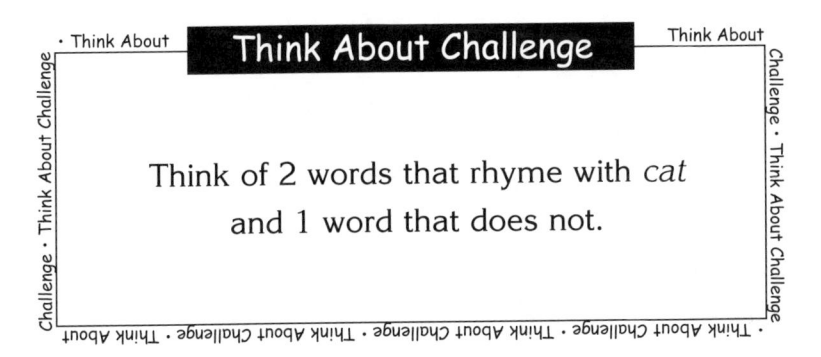

ea • s • t   *s • t • e • p*   *c • l • a • ss*

p • r • e • ss   *c • l • i • mb*   *d • r • i • p*

Think About Challenge

Think of 2 words that rhyme with *cat* and 1 word that does not.

Phonological Awareness

Workout #7

> 👆 When pronouncing an italicized letter (e.g., *t*), be sure to pronounce it by the sound it makes, rather than saying its letter name *(tee)* or adding a vowel to it *(ta)*.

Segmenting Syllables

Say a sentence with:

    3 parts (syllables)

    4 parts (syllables)

    5 parts (syllables)

Rhyming

Which word does not rhyme?

    tip, **tap,** *rip*   *cry, sigh,* **soap**

    tooth, booth, **bath**   *playing,* **trying,** *saying*

    one, *toe, low*   *dog, smog,* **lag**

Blending Sounds

Does *w • i • gg • le* say *wiggle?* (Y)

Does *b • a • b • y* say *maybe?* (N)

Does *h • o • ll • y* say *holly?* (Y)

Does *t • i • n • y* say *timely?* (N)

Does *s • o • d • a* say *cola?* (N)

Workout #7

Segmenting Sounds in Words

Do these words begin with the same sound?

    lotion, loose (Y)   *chip, chin* (Y)   *bath, path* (N)

    south, zoom (N)   *find, fool* (Y)   *month, money* (Y)

Manipulating Sounds

Say *da*. Now add a *k* sound to the end of *da*. *(dock)*

Say *addle*. Now add a *p* sound to the beginning of *addle*. *(paddle)*

Say *ar*. Now add a *t* sound to the end of *ar*. *(art)*

Say *free*. Now add a *z* sound to the end of *free*. *(freeze)*

Say *ant*. Now add a *k* sound to the beginning of *ant*. *(can't)*

Working with Clusters

Say *blue*. Now say *blue* without the *b* sound. *(Lou)*

Say *slush*. Now say *slush* without the *s* sound. *(lush)*

Say *queen*. Now say *queen* without the *k* sound. *(ween)*

Say *plea*. Now say *plea* without the *p* sound. *(Lee)*

Say *trees*. Now say *trees* without the *r* sound. *(tease)*

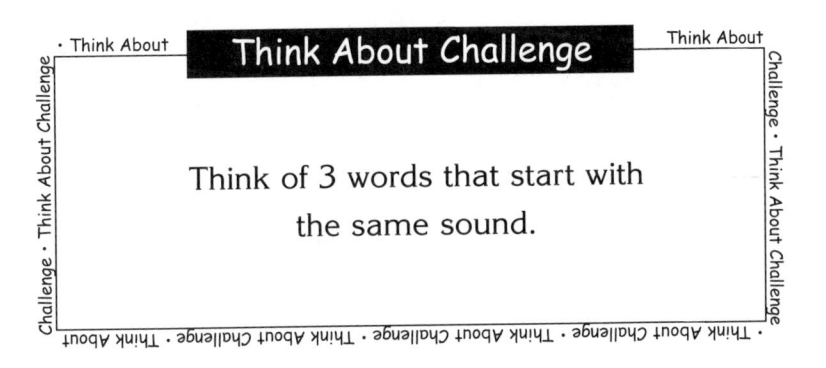

Think About Challenge

Think of 3 words that start with the same sound.

Phonological Awareness
Workout #8

> 👉 When pronouncing an italicized letter (e.g., *t*), be sure to pronounce it by the sound it makes, rather than saying its letter name *(tee)* or adding a vowel to it *(ta)*.

Segmenting Syllables

Say *backyard*. Now say *backyard* without *back*. *(yard)*
Say *dragonfly*. Now say *dragonfly* without *fly*. *(dragon)*
Say *dollhouse*. Now say *dollhouse* without *doll*. *(house)*
Say *hot dog*. Now say *hot dog* without *dog*. *(hot)*
Say *softball*. Now say *softball* without *soft*. *(ball)*

Rhyming

Which of these words rhymes with
    snip: *snap, step,* or ***tip?***
    hint: *hunt,* ***mint,*** or *him?*
    clawed: *cat,* ***sawed,*** or *fruit?*
    wiggle: *going,* ***giggle,*** or *tickle?*
    pat: *comb, love,* or ***sat?***

Blending Syllables

Blend these parts (syllables) together. What word do they make?

    u • ni • for • mi • ty   *un • ques • tion • a • ble*
    ter • mi • nol • o • gy   *tra • di • tion • al • ly*
    in • ves • ti • ga • tive   *au • di • ol • o • gist*

Workout #8

Segmenting Sounds in Words

Does this word have 3 sounds?

    beat (Y)   *pet* (Y)   *work* (Y)

    popped (N)   *key* (N)   *map* (Y)

Manipulating Sounds

Say *went*. Now say *went* without the ending sound. *(when)*

Say *right*. Now say *right* without the ending sound. *(rye)*

Say *gleam*. Now say *gleam* without the ending sound. *(glee)*

Say *stone*. Now say *stone* without the ending sound. *(stow)*

Say *groan*. Now say *groan* without the ending sound. *(grow)*

Working with Clusters

Say *trip*. Now say *trip* without the *t* sound. *(rip)*

Say *grim*. Now say *grim* without the *g* sound. *(rim)*

Say *blip*. Now say *blip* without the *b* sound. *(lip)*

Say *pride*. Now say *pride* without the *p* sound. *(ride)*

Say *stop*. Now say *stop* without the *s* sound. *(top)*

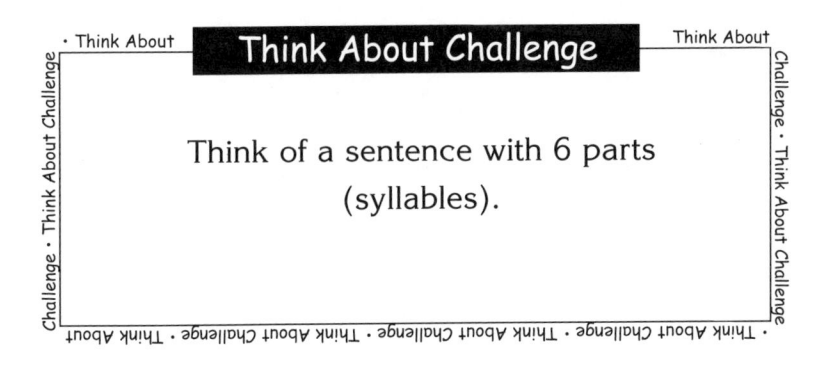

Think About Challenge

Think of a sentence with 6 parts (syllables).

Phonological Awareness
Workout #9

> 👉 When pronouncing an italicized letter (e.g., *t*), be sure to pronounce it by the sound it makes, rather than saying its letter name *(tee)* or adding a vowel to it *(ta)*.

Segmenting Syllables

Clap out the parts (syllables) in the word:

September (3)	*medicine* (3)
brontosaurus (4)	*saltwater* (3)
intersection (4)	*precipitation* (5)

Rhyming

Give a word that rhymes with:

blink	*fizzy*	*squirrel*
wand	*twist*	*zippy*

Blending Sounds

Does *b • ou • n • c • ed* say *boys* or **bounced?**

Does *a • nn • u • a • l* say **annual** or *manual?*

Does *b • e • c • au • se* say **because** or *bicuspid?*

Does *p • o • l • i • sh* say *abolish* or **polish?**

Does *b • a • ll • oo • n* say *baboon* or **balloon?**

Workout #9

Segmenting Sounds in Words

Do you hear a *th* sound in this word?

    thumb (Y)   *thunder* (Y)   *fender* (N)
    pathway (Y)   *shine* (N)   *path* (Y)

Manipulating Sounds

Say *red*. Now say *red* without the beginning sound. *(Ed)*
Say *doughnut*. Now say *doughnut* without the beginning sound. *(oughnut)*
Say *silent*. Now say *silent* without the beginning sound. *(ilent)*
Say *gooey*. Now say *gooey* without the beginning sound. *(ooey)*
Say *super*. Now say *super* without the beginning sound. *(uper)*

Working with Clusters

How many sounds do you hear in the word:

    fly (3)   *play* (3)   *pink* (4)
    thread (4)   *smile* (4)   *fries* (4)

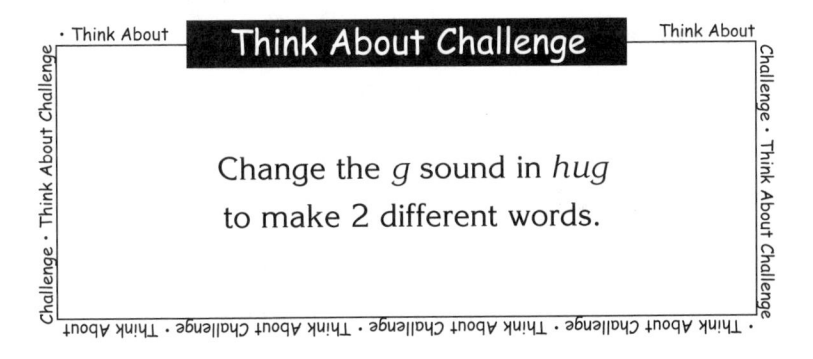

Think About Challenge

Change the *g* sound in *hug* to make 2 different words.

Phonological Awareness

Workout #10

> 👉 When pronouncing an italicized letter (e.g., *t*), be sure to pronounce it by the sound it makes, rather than saying its letter name *(tee)* or adding a vowel to it *(ta)*.

Segmenting Syllables

Tell how many parts (syllables) are in the whole sentence:

The dog is fast. (4)

He likes pizza. (4)

Her name is Elizabeth. (7)

It is snowing outside. (6)

The truck is going fast. (6)

Rhyming

Fill in the blank with a rhyming word.

Old Mother *Hubbard* went to her _____.

Jack and *Jill* went up the _____.

Mirror, Mirror, on the *wall,* who is the fairest one of _____?

Turn that *frown* upside _____.

The rain in *Spain* falls mainly on the _____.

Blending Syllables

Blend these parts (syllables) together. What word do they make?

part • ly   tunn • el   clear • ance

star • tle   rea • der   cu • ckoo

Workout #10

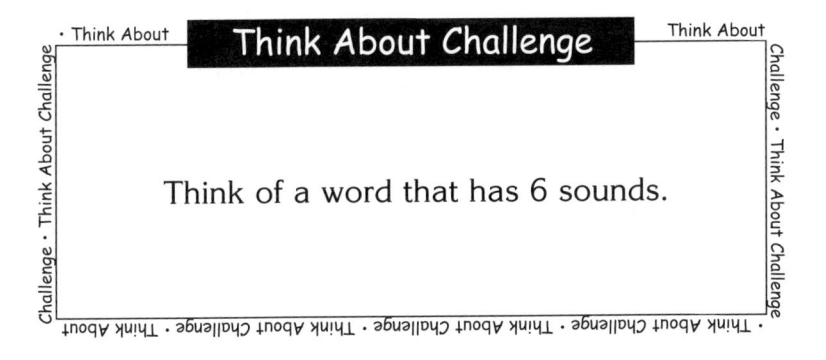

Segmenting Sounds in Words

What sound does this word begin with, *p* or *b?*

    purple   *burnt*   *bubble*

    police   *pony*   *baggy*

Manipulating Sounds

Say *tin*. Now say *tin* with a *b* sound instead of the *t* sound. *(bin)*

Say *cane*. Now say *cane* with a *l* sound instead of the *k* sound. *(lane)*

Say *dice*. Now say *dice* with a *r* sound instead of the *d* sound. *(rice)*

Say *rake*. Now say *rake* with a *f* sound instead of the *r* sound. *(fake)*

Say *pool*. Now say *pool* with a *k* sound instead of the *p* sound. *(cool)*

Working with Clusters

Does this word end with *mp?*

    mint (N)   *lamp* (Y)   *runt* (N)

    stomp (Y)   *chimp* (Y)   *rim* (N)

Think About Challenge

Think of a word that has 6 sounds.

Phonological Awareness

Workout #11

> ☞ When pronouncing an italicized letter (e.g., *t*), be sure to pronounce it by the sound it makes, rather than saying its letter name *(tee)* or adding a vowel to it *(ta)*.

Segmenting Syllables

Are there 3 or 4 parts (syllables) in the word *barbecue?* (3)

Are there 4 or 5 parts (syllables) in the word *celebration?* (4)

Are there 3 or 4 parts (syllables) in the word *librarian?* (4)

Are there 2 or 3 parts (syllables) in the word *umbrella?* (3)

Are there 3 or 4 parts (syllables) in the word *accordion?* (4)

Rhyming

Do these two words rhyme?

jug, bug (Y)   *belt, bell* (N)   *tank, rink* (N)

birch, church (Y)   *spoon, room* (N)   *pocket, locket* (Y)

Blending Sounds

Does *p • i • ll • ow* say *pill* or **pillow?**

Does *s • a • g • a* say *sagging* or **saga?**

Does *B • o • bb • y* say **Bobby** or *mommy?*

Does *h • u • l • a* say **hula** or *ruler?*

Does *h • e • nn • a* say *hen* or **henna?**

Workout #11

Segmenting Sounds in Words

Think of a word that ends with:

sh	m	b
z	t	n

Manipulating Sounds

Say *ap*. Now add a *t* sound to the beginning of *ap*. *(tap)*
Say *ip*. Now add a *s* sound to the beginning of *ip*. *(sip)*
Say *ash*. Now add a *k* sound to the beginning of *ash*. *(cash)*
Say *an*. Now add a *t* sound to the beginning of *an*. *(tan)*
Say *of*. Now add a *l* sound to the beginning of *of*. *(love)*

Working with Clusters

Say *trial*. Now say *trial* without the beginning sound. *(rile)*
Say *slightly*. Now say *slightly* without the beginning sound. *(lightly)*
Say *greeting*. Now say *greeting* without the beginning sound. *(reeting)*
Say *dry*. Now say *dry* without the beginning sound. *(rye)*
Say *Fred*. Now say *Fred* without the beginning sound. *(red)*

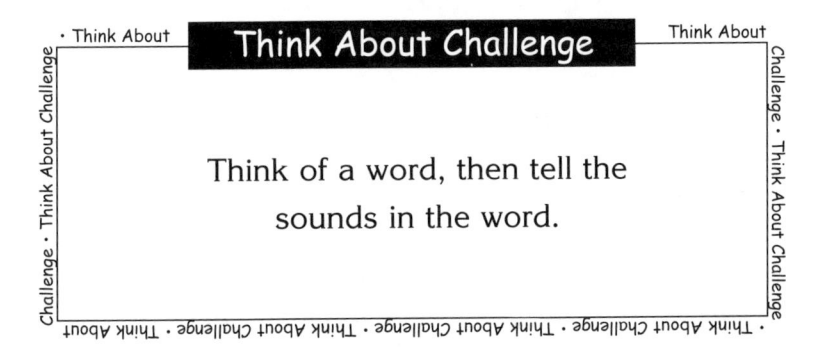

Think About Challenge

Think of a word, then tell the sounds in the word.

Phonological Awareness

Workout #12

> ☞ When pronouncing an italicized letter (e.g., *t*), be sure to pronounce it by the sound it makes, rather than saying its letter name *(tee)* or adding a vowel to it *(ta)*.

Segmenting Syllables

Give a word that has:
- 2 parts (syllables)
- 3 parts (syllables)
- 4 parts (syllables)

Rhyming

Which of these words rhymes with

trap: *trip, cape,* or **strap?**

cane: *can,* **mane,** or *game?*

leap: **peep,** *man,* or *soap?*

gave: *glove,* **save,** or *hinge?*

ham: *sun,* **slam,** or *home?*

Blending Syllables

Blend these parts (syllables) together. What word do they make?

nev • er • the • less   *di • ver • si • ty*

u • ni • ver • sal   *con • ver • sa • tion*

gen • e • ra • tion   *cau • li • flow • er*

Workout #12

Segmenting Sounds in Words

Does this word begin with a *f* sound?

    find (Y)   *fender* (Y)   *vandal* (N)

    baby (N)   *voice* (N)   *wipe* (N)

Manipulating Sounds

Say *trees*, then say *tree*. What sound makes these two words different? *(z)*

Say *fee*, then say *feet*. What sound makes these two words different? *(t)*

Say *row*, then say *rope*. What sound makes these two words different? *(p)*

Say *why*, then say *whine*. What sound makes these two words different? *(n)*

Say *tie*, then say *tight*. What sound makes these two words different? *(t)*

Working with Clusters

What are the sounds in the word:

    fright   *clipped*   *cloak*

    drags   *smile*   *stocking*

Think About Challenge

Think of word with 4 parts (syllables) that begins with a *m* sound.

Phonological Awareness

Workout #13

> ☞ When pronouncing an italicized letter (e.g., *t*), be sure to pronounce it by the sound it makes, rather than saying its letter name *(tee)* or adding a vowel to it *(ta)*.

Segmenting Syllables

Say *cupcake*. Now say *cupcake* without *cup*. *(cake)*

Say *campground*. Now say *campground* without *ground*. *(camp)*

Say *jellyfish*. Now say *jellyfish* without *jelly*. *(fish)*

Say *football*. Now say *football* without *ball*. *(foot)*

Say *jump rope*. Now say *jump rope* without *jump*. *(rope)*

Rhyming

Give 3 words that rhyme with:

zip	*pound*	*spend*
jug	*swat*	*flipping*

Blending Sounds

Blend these sounds together. What word do they make?

g • u • t	*l • i • ne*	*c • ou • ld*
h • a • ve	*t • a • me*	*r • u • de*

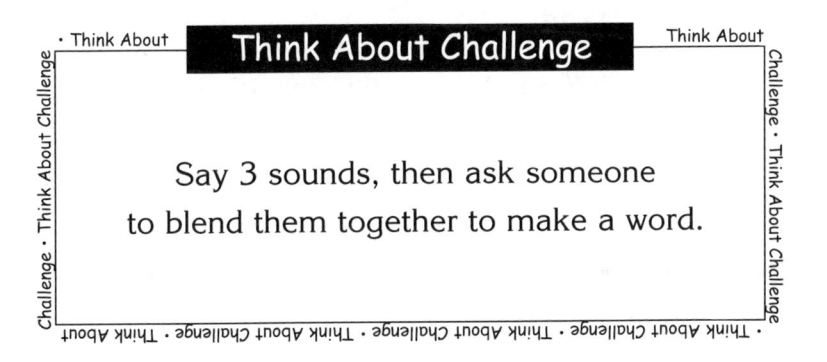

Workout #13

Segmenting Sounds in Words

What sound does this word end with, *t* or *d?*

    pat   *slide*   *knot*

    wide   *code*   *mad*

Manipulating Sounds

Say *sigh*. Now add a *n* sound to the end of *sigh*. *(sign)*

Say *ox*. Now add a *b* sound to the beginning of *ox*. *(box)*

Say *sly*. Now add a *d* sound to the end of *sly*. *(slide)*

Say *ounce*. Now add a *p* sound to the beginning of *ounce*. *(pounce)*

Say *ill*. Now add a *j* sound to the beginning of *ill*. *(Jill)*

Working with Clusters

What two sounds does this word end with, *st* or *ts?*

    blast   *pots*   *mist*

    kissed (st)   *gust*   *rats*

Think About Challenge

Say 3 sounds, then ask someone to blend them together to make a word.

Phonological Awareness

Workout #14

> 👉 When pronouncing an italicized letter (e.g., *t*), be sure to pronounce it by the sound it makes, rather than saying its letter name *(tee)* or adding a vowel to it *(ta)*.

Segmenting Syllables

Say a sentence with:

- 4 parts (syllables)
- 5 parts (syllables)
- 6 parts (syllables)

Rhyming

Give a word that rhymes with:

| *spin* | *germ* | *shore* |
| *grip* | *won* | *line* |

Blending Syllables

Does *con • grat • u • la • tions* say **congratulations** or *graduations?*

Does *mod • i • fi • ca • tion* say **modification** or *modulation?*

Does *in • ves • ti • ga • tion* say **investigation** or *invest?*

Does *ac • cel • e • ra • tor* say *acceleration* or **accelerator?**

Does *au • then • tic • i • ty* say *ethnicity* or **authenticity?**

Workout #14

Segmenting Sounds in Words

Think of a word that begins with:

h	m	z
b	k	ch

Manipulating Sounds

Say *dial*. Now say *dial* without the ending sound. *(die)*
Say *drive*. Now say *drive* without the ending sound. *(dry)*
Say *goose*. Now say *goose* without the ending sound. *(goo)*
Say *leaf*. Now say *leaf* without the ending sound. *(Lee)*
Say *rise*. Now say *rise* without the ending sound. *(rye)*

Working with Clusters

Say *best*, then say *bet*. What sound makes these two words different? *(s)*

Say *pump*, then say *pup*. What sound makes these two words different? *(m)*

Say *fund*, then say *fun*. What sound makes these two words different? *(d)*

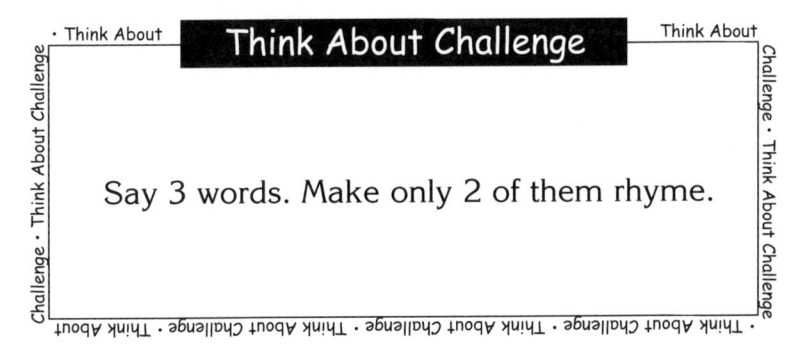

Say *lilt*, then say *lit*. What sound makes these two words different? *(l)*

Say *sand*, then say *sad*. What sound makes these two words different? *(n)*

Think About Challenge

Say 3 words. Make only 2 of them rhyme.

Phonological Awareness

Workout #15

> ☞ When pronouncing an italicized letter (e.g., *t*), be sure to pronounce it by the sound it makes, rather than saying its letter name *(tee)* or adding a vowel to it *(ta)*.

Segmenting Syllables

Clap out the parts (syllables) in the word:

    uppercase (3)   *abbreviation* (5)

    October (3)   *exclamation* (4)

    illustrator (4)   *paragraph* (3)

Rhyming

Give 2 words that rhyme with:

    tub   *jet*   *pop*

    clock   *quick*   *dish*

Blending Sounds

Blend these sounds together. What word do they make?

    t • *oo* • *k*   *v* • *a* • *se*   *s* • *a* • *ve*

    n • *i* • *ne*   *kn* • *i* • *fe*   *sh* • *i* • *n*

Workout #15

Segmenting Sounds in Words

Think of a word that begins with the same sound as:

    six   *miss*   *bone*

    nice   *wind*   *chime*

Manipulating Sounds

Say *fence*. Now say *fence* without the beginning sound. *(ence)*

Say *dance*. Now say *dance* without the beginning sound. *(ants)*

Say *hitch*. Now say *hitch* without the beginning sound. *(itch)*

Say *mop*. Now say *mop* without the beginning sound. *(op)*

Say *yup*. Now say *yup* without the beginning sound. *(up)*

Working with Clusters

Say *rug*. Now add a *z* sound to the end of *rug*. *(rugs)*

Say *wagon*. Now add a *z* sound to the end of *wagon*. *(wagons)*

Say *smell*. Now add a *t* sound to the end of *smell*. *(smelt)*

Say *rock*. Now add a *t* sound to the end of *rock*. *(rocked)*

Say *hum*. Now add a *p* sound to the end of *hum*. *(hump)*

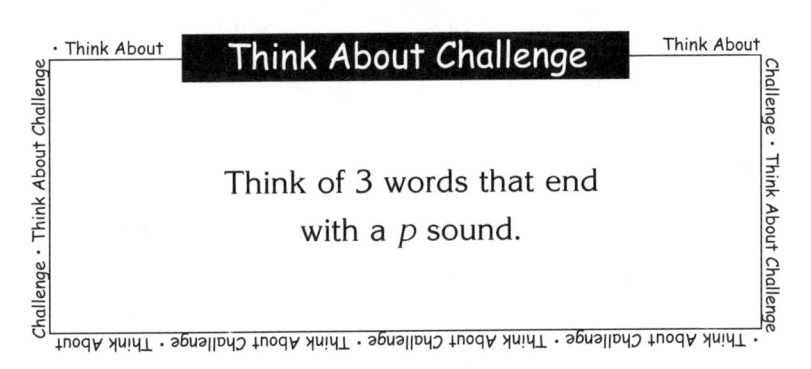

Think About Challenge

Think of 3 words that end with a *p* sound.

Phonological Awareness
Workout #16

> 👉 When pronouncing an italicized letter (e.g., *t*), be sure to pronounce it by the sound it makes, rather than saying its letter name *(tee)* or adding a vowel to it *(ta)*.

Segmenting Syllables

Tell how many parts (syllables) are in the whole sentence:

His name is Fred. (4)

The baby is hungry. (6)

The phone is ringing. (5)

It is time to eat. (5)

Go to your bedroom. (5)

Rhyming

Give a word that rhymes with:

braces	*winking*	*phone*
floor	*shows*	*pink*

Blending Sounds

Blend these sounds together. What word do they make?

s • u • sh • i	*a • tt • i • c*	*t • i • d • y*
c • o • ff • ee	*d • i • nn • er*	*r • u • b • y*

Workout #16

Segmenting Sounds in Words

What sounds do you hear in this word?

fit   *did*   *heat*

dug   *comb*   *rock*

Manipulating Sounds

Say *oot*. Now add a *b* sound to the beginning of *oot*. *(boot)*

Say *I'm*. Now add a *t* sound to the beginning of *I'm*. *(time)*

Say *oaf*. Now add a *l* sound to the beginning of *oaf*. *(loaf)*

Say *ending*. Now add a *s* sound to the beginning of *ending*. *(sending)*

Say *inner*. Now add a *th* sound to the beginning of *inner*. *(thinner)*

Working with Clusters

Does this word begin with *pl*?

purple (N)   *plastic* (Y)   *pickle* (N)

please (Y)   *play* (Y)   *pride* (N)

Think About Challenge

Think of 2 words that are the same except for 1 sound.

Phonological Awareness
Workout #17

> ☞ When pronouncing an italicized letter (e.g., *t*), be sure to pronounce it by the sound it makes, rather than saying its letter name *(tee)* or adding a vowel to it *(ta)*.

Segmenting Syllables

Are there 3 or 4 parts (syllables) in the word *hummingbird?* (3)

Are there 4 or 5 parts (syllables) in the word *vegetarian?* (5)

Are there 3 or 4 parts (syllables) in the word *cranberry?* (3)

Are there 2 or 3 parts (syllables) in the word *orange?* (2)

Are there 3 or 4 parts (syllables) in the word *microwave?* (3)

Rhyming

Which word does not rhyme?

    pike, bike, **bite**   **pal,** *far, car*

    beg, Meg, **bag**   **drop,** *tip, slip*

    tent, *ten, spent*   *elves,* **elf,** *shelves*

Blending Syllables

Blend these parts (syllables) together. What word do they make?

    litt • er • bug   *sen • si • tive*   *sil • ver • ware*

    re • cit • al   *va • can • cy*   *in • sult • ed*

Workout #17

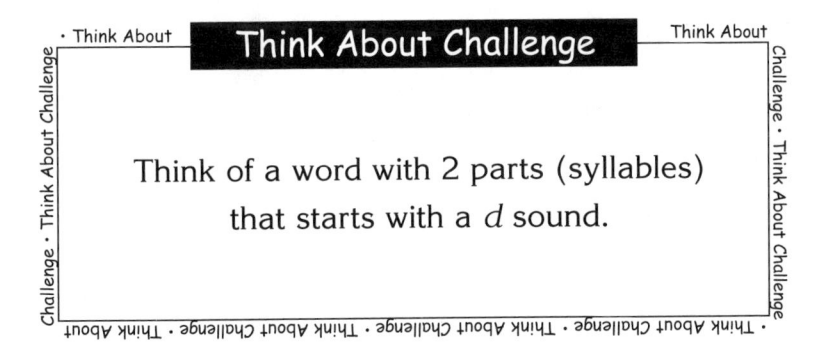

Segmenting Sounds in Words

How many sounds do you hear in the word:

size (3)   *push* (3)   *up* (2)
set (3)   *with* (3)   *sheep* (3)

Manipulating Sounds

Say *bar*. Now add a *n* sound to the end of *bar*. *(barn)*
Say *par*. Now add a *t* sound to the end of *par*. *(part)*
Say *gray*. Now add a *d* sound to the end of *gray*. *(grade)*
Say *rah*. Now add a *b* sound to the end of *rah*. *(rob)*
Say *core*. Now add a *d* sound to the end of *core*. *(cord)*

Working with Clusters

Say *gripe*, then say *ripe*. What sound makes these two words different? *(g)*
Say *group*, then say *goop*. What sound makes these two words different? *(r)*
Say *stable*, then say *table*. What sound makes these two words different? *(s)*
Say *sting*, then say *sing*. What sound makes these two words different? *(t)*
Say *stable*, then say *sable*. What sound makes these two words different? *(t)*

Think About Challenge

Think of a word with 2 parts (syllables) that starts with a *d* sound.

Phonological Awareness
Workout #18

> ☞ When pronouncing an italicized letter (e.g., *t*), be sure to pronounce it by the sound it makes, rather than saying its letter name *(tee)* or adding a vowel to it *(ta)*.

Segmenting Syllables

Tell the number of parts (syllables) in the word(s):

newspaper (3)   *Arizona* (4)

sunglasses (3)   *pediatrician* (5)

banana split (4)   *television* (4)

Rhyming

Give 3 words that rhyme with:

pop   *egg*   *clap*

jug   *top*   *smear*

Blending Sounds

Does *b* • *a* • *ll* say *ball*? (Y)

Does *d* • *i* • *me* say *time*? (N)

Does *w* • *or* • *d* say *worm*? (N)

Does *b* • *i* • *b* say *big*? (N)

Does *b* • *u* • *g* say *buck*? (N)

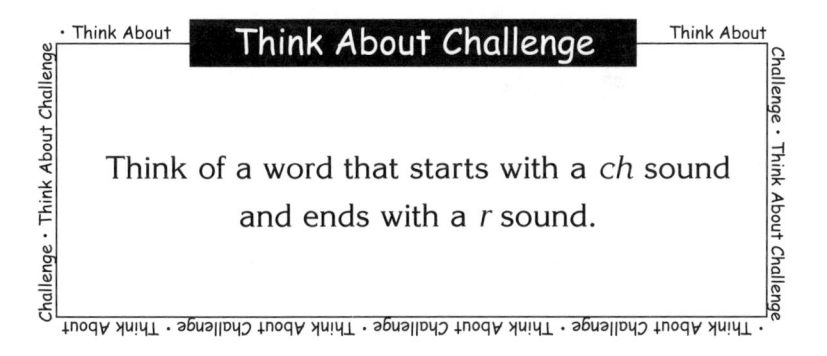

Workout #18

Segmenting Sounds in Words

Does this word have 3 sounds?

banjo (N)	*shame* (Y)	*will* (Y)
bus (Y)	*seat* (Y)	*go* (N)

Manipulating Sounds

Say *lap*. Now say *lap* with a ĭ sound instead of the ă sound. *(lip)*

Say *hot*. Now say *hot* with a ă sound instead of the ŏ sound. *(hat)*

Say *chick*. Now say *chick* with a ō sound instead of the ĭ sound. *(choke)*

Say *cup*. Now say *cup* with a o͞o sound instead of the ŭ sound. *(coop)*

Say *well*. Now say *well* with a ī sound instead of the ĕ sound. *(while)*

Working with Clusters

Think of a word that begins with:

tr	bl	kr
thr	pr	skr

Think About Challenge

Think of a word that starts with a *ch* sound and ends with a *r* sound.

Phonological Awareness
Workout #19

☞ When pronouncing an italicized letter (e.g., *t*), be sure to pronounce it by the sound it makes, rather than saying its letter name *(tee)* or adding a vowel to it *(ta)*.

Segmenting Syllables

Say *cowboy*. Now say *cowboy* without *cow*. *(boy)*

Say *flower bed*. Now say *flower bed* without *bed*. *(flower)*

Say *snowman*. Now say *snowman* without *man*. *(snow)*

Say *ice cream*. Now say *ice cream* without *cream*. *(ice)*

Say *rainbow*. Now say *rainbow* without *rain*. *(bow)*

Rhyming

Give 3 words that rhyme with:

fell	*oat*	*shop*
lock	*horn*	*flew*

Blending Sounds

Blend these sounds together. What word do they make?

r • o • t • a • te   *r • e • c • i • te*

wr • i • tt • e • n   *l • i • st • e • n*

g • a • ll • o • p   *t • a • nn • i • ng*

Workout #19

Segmenting Sounds in Words

Do these words begin with the same sound?

    sugar, ship (Y)   car, jump (N)   home, wood (N)

    pen, pig (Y)   hat, hammer (Y)   mitt, mouse (Y)

Manipulating Sounds

Say *at*. Now add a *k* sound to the beginning of *at*. *(cat)*

Say *why*. Now add a *d* sound to the end of *why*. *(wide)*

Say *tie*. Now add a *p* sound to the end of *tie*. *(type)*

Say *buy*. Now add a *d* sound to the end of *buy*. *(bide)*

Say *up*. Now add a *p* sound to the beginning of *up*. *(pup)*

Working with Clusters

Say *rap*. Now add a *t* sound to the beginning of *rap*. *(trap)*

Say *lap*. Now add a *s* sound to the beginning of *lap*. *(slap)*

Say *lash*. Now add a *k* sound to the beginning of *lash*. *(clash)*

Say *car*. Now add a *s* sound to the beginning of *car*. *(scar)*

Say *love*. Now add a *g* sound to the beginning of *love*. *(glove)*

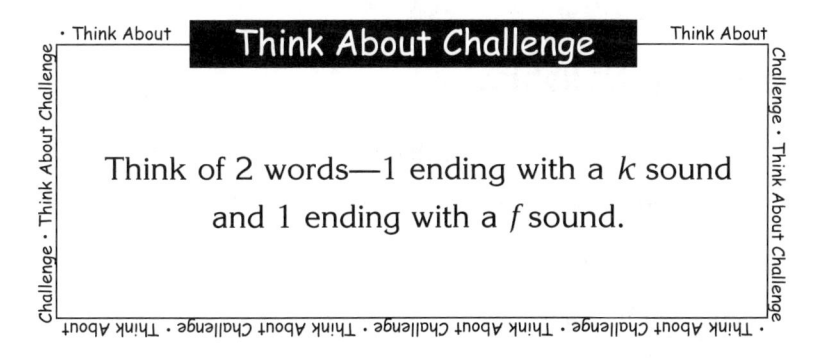

Think About Challenge

Think of 2 words—1 ending with a *k* sound and 1 ending with a *f* sound.

Phonological Awareness
Workout #20

> 👉 When pronouncing an italicized letter (e.g., *t*), be sure to pronounce it by the sound it makes, rather than saying its letter name *(tee)* or adding a vowel to it *(ta)*.

Segmenting Syllables

Tap out the parts (syllables) in the word:

    basketball (3)   *kindergarten* (4)   *cafeteria* (5)

    Colorado (4)   *radio* (3)   *underwater* (4)

Rhyming

Which word does not rhyme?

    green, clean, **grin**   *price, dice,* **light**

    teach, **blush**, *reach*   *book,* **put**, *hook*

    candy, *candle, handle*   *sour,* **paper**, *power*

Blending Syllables

Blend these parts (syllables) together. What word do they make?

    cel • e • bra • tion   thun • der • show • er

    Cal • i • forn • ia   ac • tiv • i • ty

    co • mmu • ni • ty   di • scov • e • ry

Workout #20

Segmenting Sounds in Words

Do these words end with the same sound?

    love, loop (N)   *hose, rise* (Y)   *queen, prince* (N)

    one, fin (Y)   *rug, big* (Y)   *star, stone* (N)

Manipulating Sounds

Say *heavy*. Now say *heavy* without the ending sound. *(heav)*

Say *pillow*. Now say *pillow* without the ending sound. *(pill)*

Say *tippy*. Now say *tippy* without the ending sound. *(tip)*

Say *solo*. Now say *solo* without the ending sound. *(sole)*

Say *sorry*. Now say *sorry* without the ending sound. *(sore)*

Working with Clusters

How many sounds do you hear in the word:

    strange (6)   *healthy* (5)   *flea* (3)

    crunch (5)   *trim* (4)   *stops* (5)

Think About Challenge

Think of 2 words that have 2 sounds alike and all other sounds different.

Phonological Awareness

Workout #21

> 👉 When pronouncing an italicized letter (e.g., *t*), be sure to pronounce it by the sound it makes, rather than saying its letter name *(tee)* or adding a vowel to it *(ta)*.

Segmenting Syllables

Clap out the parts (syllables) in the word:

Florida (3)   *tyrannosaurus* (5)

video (3)   *buttercup* (3)

Cinderella (4)   *saxophone* (3)

Rhyming

Do these two words rhyme?

bite, bike (N)   *happy, snappy* (Y)

please, knees (Y)   *square, bear* (Y)

drink, sink (Y)   *ocean, lotion* (Y)

Blending Sounds

Does *m • i • ss* say **miss** or *mist?*

Does *p • o • le* say *bowl* or **pole?**

Does *sh • i • p* say **ship** or *shop?*

Does *n • a • me* say **name** or *aim?*

Does *th • e • m* say **them** or *theme?*

Workout #21

Segmenting Sounds in Words

Does this word end with a *n* sound?

| *bin* (Y) | *pine* (Y) | *time* (N) |
| *noise* (N) | *fame* (N) | *tin* (Y) |

Manipulating Sounds

Say *John*. Now say *John* without the beginning sound. *(on)*
Say *lip*. Now say *lip* without the beginning sound. *(ip)*
Say *tie*. Now say *tie* without the beginning sound. *(I)*
Say *top*. Now say *top* without the beginning sound. *(op)*
Say *win*. Now say *win* without the beginning sound. *(in)*

Working with Clusters

Say *pry*. Now say *pry* with a *k* sound instead of the *p* sound. *(cry)*
Say *climb*. Now say *climb* with a *s* sound instead of the *k* sound. *(slime)*
Say *cling*. Now say *cling* with a *p* sound instead of the *k* sound. *(pling)*
Say *crate*. Now say *crate* with a *g* sound instead of the *k* sound. *(grate)*
Say *grab*. Now say *grab* with a *d* sound instead of the *g* sound. *(drab)*

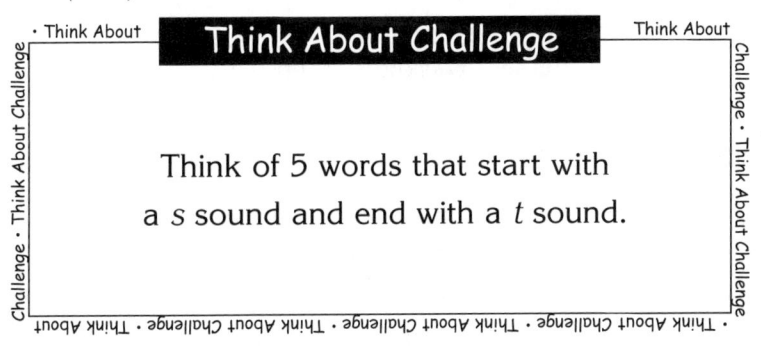

Think About Challenge

Think of 5 words that start with a *s* sound and end with a *t* sound.

Phonological Awareness
Workout #22

> ✋ When pronouncing an italicized letter (e.g., *t*), be sure to pronounce it by the sound it makes, rather than saying its letter name *(tee)* or adding a vowel to it *(ta)*.

Segmenting Syllables

Tell how many parts (syllables) are in the whole sentence:
The brownie is hot. (5)
My mother is sleeping. (6)
Jacob's tower fell down. (6)
Yesterday I was sick. (6)
The rain will fall tomorrow. (7)

Rhyming

Fill in the blank with a rhyming word.
Jack *Sprat* could eat no _____.
This is the church; this is the *steeple*. Open the doors, and see all the _____.
Paul, Paul, he's our *man*. If he can't do it, no one _____.
It's raining. It's *pouring*. The old man is _____.
Cinderella, dressed in *yellow*, went upstairs to kiss a _____.

Blending Syllables

Does *mys • ti • cal* say **mystical** or *mythical*?
Does *cu • bi • cle* say *cuticle* or **cubicle**?
Does *de • ter • gent* say *deterrent* or **detergent**?
Does *trans • la • tion* say **translation** or *transmission*?
Does *ra • di • o* say **radio** or *radius*?

Workout #22

Segmenting Sounds in Words

Think of a word that begins with:

| l | th | p |
| v | g | w |

Manipulating Sounds

Say *ite*. Now add a *t* sound to the beginning of *ite*. *(tight)*
Say *add*. Now add a *b* sound to the beginning of *add*. *(bad)*
Say *ight*. Now add a *b* sound to the beginning of *ight*. *(bite)*
Say *ap*. Now add a *s* sound to the beginning of *ap*. *(sap)*
Say *ump*. Now add a *l* sound to the beginning of *ump*. *(lump)*

Working with Clusters

Say *bar*. Now add a *n* sound to the end of *bar*. *(barn)*
Say *par*. Now add a *t* sound to the end of *par*. *(part)*
Say *gran*. Now add a *d* sound to the end of *gran*. *(grand)*
Say *ran*. Now add a *t* sound to the end of *ran*. *(rant)*
Say *core*. Now add a *z* sound to the end of *core*. *(cores)*

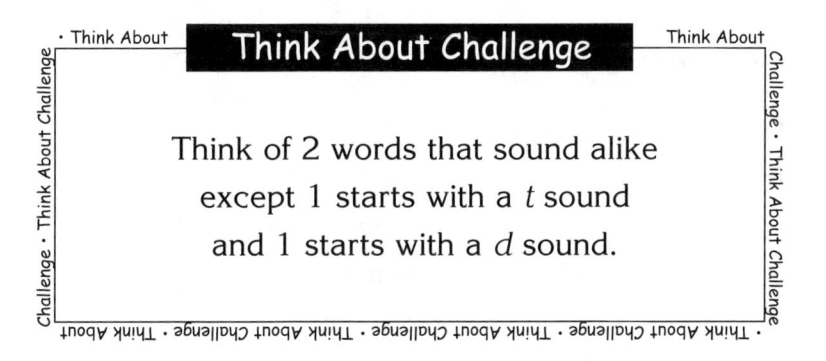

Think About Challenge

Think of 2 words that sound alike except 1 starts with a *t* sound and 1 starts with a *d* sound.

79

Phonological Awareness

Workout #23

☞ When pronouncing an italicized letter (e.g., *t*), be sure to pronounce it by the sound it makes, rather than saying its letter name *(tee)* or adding a vowel to it *(ta)*.

Segmenting Syllables

Tell the number of parts (syllables) in the word(s):

Louisiana (5)   *capital* (3)

watermelon (4)   *seventeen* (3)

birthday party (4)   *family* (3)

Rhyming

Do these two words rhyme?

choice, voice (Y)   *huddle, cuddle* (Y)

less, left (N)   *beard, heard* (N)

fervent, servant (Y)   *tangle, tingle* (N)

Blending Syllables

Does *ba • nan • a* say *bunny* or **banana?**

Does *pop • si • cle* say *bicycle* or **popsicle?**

Does *pho • to • graph* say *phonograph* or **photograph?**

Does *eve • ry • day* say **everyday** or *everybody?*

Does *cel • e • ry* say *celebration* or **celery?**

Workout #23

Segmenting Sounds in Words

Does this word begin with a *v* sound?

    van (Y)   *bike* (N)   *vase* (Y)

    vine (Y)   *fence* (N)   *win* (N)

Manipulating Sounds

Say *how*, then say *house*. What sound was added to *how* to make *house*? *(s)*

Say *he*, then say *heat*. What sound was added to *he* to make *heat*? *(t)*

Say *in*, then say *shin*. What sound was added to *in* to make *shin*? *(sh)*

Say *oats*, then say *coats*. What sound was added to *oats* to make *coats*? *(k)*

Say *key*, then say *keep*. What sound was added to *key* to make *keep*? *(p)*

Working with Clusters

Does this word have 4 sounds?

    slide (Y)   *spine* (Y)   *grime* (Y)

    snapped (N)   *brick* (Y)   *slipper* (N)

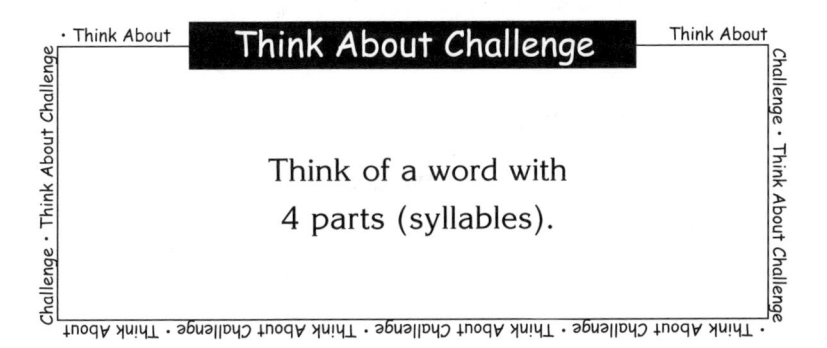

Think About Challenge

Think of a word with 4 parts (syllables).

Phonological Awareness
Workout #24

> 👉 When pronouncing an italicized letter (e.g., *t*), be sure to pronounce it by the sound it makes, rather than saying its letter name *(tee)* or adding a vowel to it *(ta)*.

Segmenting Syllables

Give a word that has:
- 3 parts (syllables)
- 4 parts (syllables)
- 5 parts (syllables)

Rhyming

Which of these words rhymes with
- *drier:* **biker**, **buyer**, or **crying**?
- *tax:* **sacks**, **ox**, or **cans**?
- *swell:* **belt**, **bell**, or **cold**?
- *bead:* **load**, **seed**, or **bus**?
- *yarn:* **barn**, **wart**, or **arm**?

Blending Sounds

Blend these sounds together. What word do they make?

p • ea • n • u • t	*p • a • ss • i • ve*
r • ai • s • i • n	*d • u • t • ie • s*
r • e • p • ea • t	*r • o • s • e • s*

Workout #24

Segmenting Sounds in Words

Do you hear a *ch* sound in this word?

swimmer (N)   *chips* (Y)   *pitch* (Y)

chime (Y)   *watches* (Y)   *ship* (N)

Manipulating Sounds

Say *wade*. Now say *wade* without the beginning sound. *(ade)*

Say *sale*. Now say *sale* without the beginning sound. *(ale)*

Say *told*. Now say *told* without the beginning sound. *(old)*

Say *lose*. Now say *lose* without the beginning sound. *(ooze)*

Say *game*. Now say *game* without the beginning sound. *(aim)*

Working with Clusters

What are the sounds in the word:

prizes   *floating*   *grilled*

bronze   *greens*   *plus*

Think About Challenge

Think of a word with 4 parts (syllables) that starts with a *m* sound.

Phonological Awareness
Workout #25

> 👉 When pronouncing an italicized letter (e.g., *t*), be sure to pronounce it by the sound it makes, rather than saying its letter name *(tee)* or adding a vowel to it *(ta)*.

Segmenting Syllables

Give a person's name that has:

    3 parts (syllables)

    4 parts (syllables)

    5 parts (syllables)

Rhyming

Give 2 words that rhyme with:

| *string* | *boat* | *line* |
| *bump* | *bread* | *cheap* |

Blending Sounds

Does *k • e • tch • u • p* say *ketchup?* (Y)

Does *r • e • m • o • te* say *remote?* (Y)

Does *m • a • r • oo • n* say *balloon?* (N)

Does *d • e • s • er • t* say *desert?* (Y)

Does *w • i • th • ou • t* say *without?* (Y)

Workout #25

Segmenting Sounds in Words

Think of a word that ends with:

l	ch	v
g	th	f

Manipulating Sounds

Say *lease*. Now say *lease* with an $\bar{\imath}$ sound instead of the $\bar{e}$ sound. *(lice)*

Say *rice*. Now say *rice* with an $\bar{a}$ sound instead of the $\bar{\imath}$ sound. *(race)*

Say *comb*. Now say *comb* with an $\bar{a}$ sound instead of the $\bar{o}$ sound. *(came)*

Say *seek*. Now say *seek* with an $\bar{o}$ sound instead of the $\bar{e}$ sound. *(soak)*

Say *pike*. Now say *pike* with an $\bar{e}$ sound instead of the $\bar{\imath}$ sound. *(peek)*

Working with Clusters

What two sounds does this word end with, *nk* or *nt*?

pant	bank	sunk
blink	splint	trunk

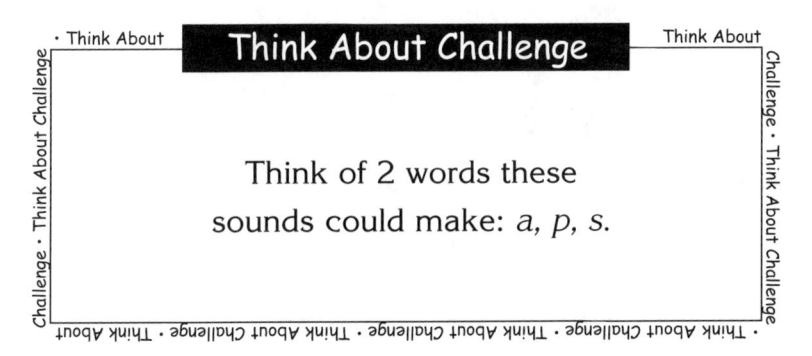

Think About Challenge

Think of 2 words these sounds could make: *a, p, s*.

85

Phonological Awareness
Workout #26

> 👉 When pronouncing an italicized letter (e.g., *t*), be sure to pronounce it by the sound it makes, rather than saying its letter name *(tee)* or adding a vowel to it *(ta)*.

Segmenting Syllables

Say a sentence with:
- 3 parts (syllables)
- 4 parts (syllables)
- 5 parts (syllables)

Rhyming

Which of these words rhymes with
- **beak:** boat, **weak,** or bat?
- **simple:** sample, **dimple,** or handy?
- **stop:** top, type, or step?
- **bending:** marble, **mending,** or getting?
- **bake: make,** pop, or train?

Blending Syllables

Blend these parts (syllables) together. What word do they make?

plen • ti • ful   gym • nas • tics
Ca • na • da   Jua • ni • ta
spoo • ki • er   maj • e • sty

Workout #26

Segmenting Sounds in Words

Think of a word that begins with the same sound as:

    cut   bed   top

    soda   chin   coat

Manipulating Sounds

Say *south*. Now say *south* without the ending sound. *(sow)*

Say *road*. Now say *road* without the ending sound. *(row)*

Say *curve*. Now say *curve* without the ending sound. *(cur)*

Say *slime*. Now say *slime* without the ending sound. *(sly)*

Say *wage*. Now say *wage* without the ending sound. *(way)*

Working with Clusters

Say *pump*. Now say *pump* without the *m* sound. *(pup)*

Say *link*. Now say *link* without the *n* sound. *(lick)*

Say *sand*. Now say *sand* without the *n* sound. *(sad)*

Say *cast*. Now say *cast* without the *s* sound. *(cat)*

Say *mix*. Now say *mix* without the *k* sound. *(miss)*

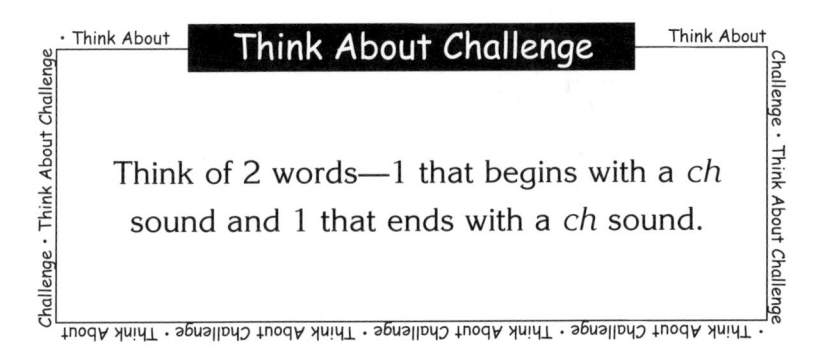

Think About Challenge

Think of 2 words—1 that begins with a *ch* sound and 1 that ends with a *ch* sound.

Phonological Awareness

Workout #27

☞ When pronouncing an italicized letter (e.g., *t*), be sure to pronounce it by the sound it makes, rather than saying its letter name *(tee)* or adding a vowel to it *(ta)*.

Segmenting Syllables

Say *shoebox*. Now say *shoebox* without *shoe*. *(box)*

Say *hairbrush*. Now say *hairbrush* without *brush*. *(hair)*

Say *notebook*. Now say *notebook* without *note*. *(book)*

Say *corn dog*. Now say *corn dog* without *corn*. *(dog)*

Say *meat loaf*. Now say *meat loaf* without *loaf*. *(meat)*

Rhyming

Give a word that rhymes with:

| *ring* | *hiker* | *bear* |
| *sand* | *lip* | *toe* |

Blending Syllables

Blend these parts (syllables) together. What word do they make?

trans • con • ti • nen • tal   *met • ro • pol • i • tan*

trig • o • nom • e • try   *opp • or • tu • ni • ty*

e • lec • tric • i • ty   *ad • min • i • stra • tion*

Workout #27

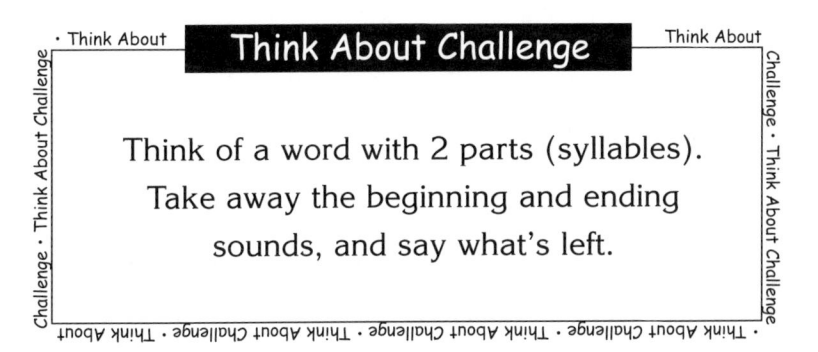

Segmenting Sounds in Words

Do these words begin with the same sound?
    soup, sand (Y)   *line, life* (Y)   *yard, year* (Y)
    done, tooth (N)   *tummy, thunder* (N) *good, cone* (N)

Manipulating Sounds

Say *lie*. Now add a *z* sound to the end of *lie*. *(lies)*
Say *hay*. Now add a *t* sound to the end of *hay*. *(hate)*
Say *jee*. Now add a *n* sound to the end of *jee*. *(jean)*
Say *toe*. Now add a *d* sound to the end of *toe*. *(toad)*
Say *flue*. Now add a *t* sound to the end of *flue*. *(flute)*

Working with Clusters

Say *strip*, then say *trip*. What sound makes these two words different? *(s)*
Say *shrine*, then say *Rhine*. What sound makes these two words different? *(sh)*
Say *thrice*, then say *rice*. What sound makes these two words different? *(th)*
Say *twine*, then say *whine*. What sound makes these two words different? *(t)*
Say *brush*, they say *rush*. What sound makes these two words different? *(b)*

Think About Challenge

Think of a word with 2 parts (syllables). Take away the beginning and ending sounds, and say what's left.

Phonological Awareness

Workout #28

☞ When pronouncing an italicized letter (e.g., *t*), be sure to pronounce it by the sound it makes, rather than saying its letter name *(tee)* or adding a vowel to it *(ta)*.

Segmenting Syllables

Give a word that has:

    2 parts (syllables)

    3 parts (syllables)

    4 parts (syllables)

Rhyming

Give 2 words that rhyme with:

| *dot* | *bill* | *weigh* |
| *ten* | *sweet* | *no* |

Blending Sounds

Blend these sounds together. What word do they make?

l • a • d • y   *ch • i • n • a*   *j • o • ck • ey*

h • or • s • ey   *k • i • w • i*   *w • i • nn • er*

Workout #28

Segmenting Sounds in Words

How many sounds do you hear in the word:

    wash (3)   *same* (3)   *shark* (3)

    on (2)   *short* (3)   *wishing* (5)

Manipulating Sounds

Say *id*. Now add a *l* sound to the beginning of *id*. *(lid)*

Say *ump*. Now add a *r* sound to the beginning of *ump*. *(rump)*

Say *pa*. Now add a *d* sound to the end of *pa*. *(pod)*

Say *ipe*. Now add a *w* sound to the beginning of *ipe*. *(wipe)*

Say *ree*. Now add a *d* sound to the end of *ree*. *(reed)*

Working with Clusters

Does this word begin with *fl*?

    friend (N)   *flutter* (Y)   *finger* (N)

    fly (Y)   *play* (N)   *flap* (Y)

Think About Challenge

Think of all the words you can that rhyme with *red*.

Phonological Awareness
Workout #29

> ☞ When pronouncing an italicized letter (e.g., *t*), be sure to pronounce it by the sound it makes, rather than saying its letter name *(tee)* or adding a vowel to it *(ta)*.

Segmenting Syllables

Clap out the parts (syllables) in the word:

wonderful (3)   *photographer* (4)

waterfall (3)   *temperature* (4)

afternoon (3)   *January* (4)

Rhyming

Give a word that rhymes with:

read   *house*   *nail*

sleep   *note*   *date*

Blending Syllables

Does *tel • e • vis • ion* say *telescope?* (N)

Does *trans • por • ta • tion* say *vacation?* (N)

Does *co • mmu • ni • cate* say *communicate?* (Y)

Does *sig • nif • i • cance* say *signature?* (N)

Does *in • de • pen • dence* say *independence?* (Y)

Workout #29

Segmenting Sounds in Words

Does this word have 3 sounds?

keeper (N)   *web* (Y)   *in* (N)

never (N)   *fork* (Y)   *knife* (Y)

Manipulating Sounds

Say *tape*. Now say *tape* without the beginning sound. *(ape)*

Say *cold*. Now say *cold* without the beginning sound. *(old)*

Say *ripe*. Now say *ripe* without the beginning sound. *(ipe)*

Say *ran*. Now say *ran* without the beginning sound. *(an)*

Say *cat*. Now say *cat* without the beginning sound. *(at)*

Working with Clusters

Say *lid*. Now add a *s* sound to the beginning of *lid*. *(slid)*

Say *rump*. Now add a *t* sound to the beginning of *rump*. *(trump)*

Say *rat*. Now add a *l* sound to the end of *rat*. *(rattle)*

Say *wipe*. Now add a *s* sound to the beginning of *wipe*. *(swipe)*

Say *read*. Now add a *z* sound to the end of *read*. *(reads)*

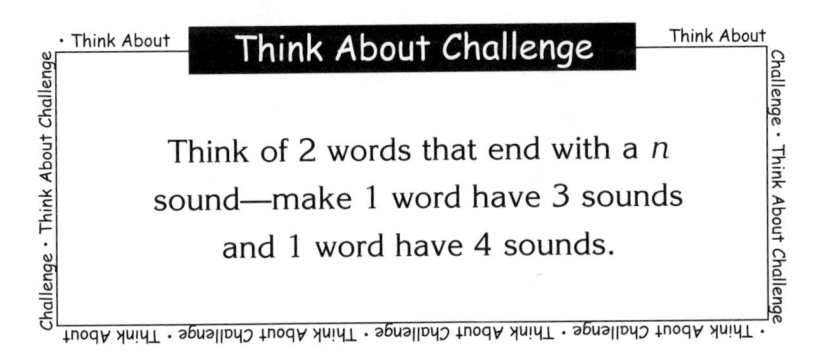

Think About Challenge

Think of 2 words that end with a *n* sound—make 1 word have 3 sounds and 1 word have 4 sounds.

Phonological Awareness

Workout #30

> ☞ When pronouncing an italicized letter (e.g., *t*), be sure to pronounce it by the sound it makes, rather than saying its letter name *(tee)* or adding a vowel to it *(ta)*.

Segmenting Syllables

Tell how many parts (syllables) are in the whole sentence:

The university is old. (8)

The kittens are eating. (6)

My leg is sore. (4)

His bicycle was stolen. (7)

Mary's dog is cute. (5)

Rhyming

Give 3 words that rhyme with:

fair	merry	dark
snack	star	go

Blending Sounds

Blend these sounds together. What word do they make?

t • u • l • i • p   *b • a • t • o • n*

f • a • sh • io • n   *s • a • l • a • d*

m • a • ch • i • ne   *r • o • ck • e • t*

Workout #30

Segmenting Sounds in Words

Do these words end with the same sound?

pit, top (N)   rot, pat (Y)   can, pin (Y)

soon, sub (N)   bed, pad (Y)   some, pill (N)

Manipulating Sounds

Say *ant*. Now add a *ch* sound to the beginning of *ant*. *(chant)*

Say *end*. Now add a *m* sound to the beginning of *end*. *(mend)*

Say *on*. Now add a *d* sound to the beginning of *on*. *(Don)*

Say *ane*. Now add a *k* sound to the beginning of *ane*. *(cane)*

Say *in*. Now add a *p* sound to the beginning of *in*. *(pin)*

Working with Clusters

How many sounds do you hear in the word:

plane (4)   pry (3)   cleaning (6)

brush (4)   scream (5)   cry (3)

Think About Challenge

Think of a word that would be very difficult to rhyme with another word.

Phonological Awareness

Workout #31

> 👉 When pronouncing an italicized letter (e.g., *t*), be sure to pronounce it by the sound it makes, rather than saying its letter name *(tee)* or adding a vowel to it *(ta)*.

Segmenting Syllables

Tell the number of parts (syllables) in the word(s):

    North America (5)   *apple pie* (3)

    monopoly (4)   *rattlesnake* (3)

    skyscraper (3)   *potato salad* (5)

Rhyming

Which word does not rhyme?

    thirty, **buddy,** *dirty*   *clue,* **fine,** *due*

    star, car, **bone**   **book,** *fire, higher*

    roar, door, **ton**   **neat,** *night, kite*

Blending Sounds

Blend these sounds together. What word do they make?

    k • ay • a • k   *g • ui • n • ea*   *v • a • p • or*

    o • p • er • a   *h • i • pp • o*   *h • e • ll • o*

Workout #31

Segmenting Sounds in Words

Does this word begin with a *t* sound?

kettle (N)   *time* (Y)   *tuna* (Y)

care (N)   *dime* (N)   *get* (N)

Manipulating Sounds

Say *cape*, then say *ape*. What sound makes these two words different? *(k)*

Say *rice*, then say *rye*. What sound makes these two words different? *(s)*

Say *nick*, then say *ick*. What sound makes these two words different? *(n)*

Say *dice*, then say *ice*. What sound makes these two words different? *(d)*

Say *gum*, then say *um*. What sound makes these two words different? *(g)*

Working with Clusters

What are the sounds in the word:

bread   *shred*   *sleeping*

slide   *spinning*   *crunchy*

Think About Challenge

Think of a word that starts with the same sound as *center*.

Phonological Awareness

Workout #32

☞ When pronouncing an italicized letter (e.g., *t*), be sure to pronounce it by the sound it makes, rather than saying its letter name *(tee)* or adding a vowel to it *(ta)*.

Segmenting Syllables

Say *doghouse*. Now say *doghouse* without *house*. *(dog)*
Say *baseball*. Now say *baseball* without *ball*. *(base)*
Say *Sunday*. Now say *Sunday* without *day*. *(sun)*
Say *hamburger*. Now say *hamburger* without *ham*. *(burger)*
Say *outside*. Now say *outside* without *out*. *(side)*

Rhyming

Give 2 words that rhyme with:

| *rent* | *Ruth* | *hook* |
| *goose* | *dog* | *sound* |

Blending Syllables

Does *ann • i • ver • sa • ry* say *nursery* or **anniversary?**
Does *per • so • nal • i • ty* say *personally* or **personality?**
Does *u • ni • ver • si • ty* say **university** or *universally?*
Does *ha • ppy • go • lu • cky* say *have to go* or **happy go lucky?**
Does *ar • tic • u • la • tion* say **articulation** or *multiplication?*

Workout #32

Segmenting Sounds in Words

Do you hear a *zh* sound in this word?

    measure (Y)   *garage* (Y)   *patch* (N)

    jump (N)   *chime* (N)   *chew* (N)

Manipulating Sounds

Say *eclair*. Now say *eclair* without the beginning sound. *(Clair)*

Say *amen*. Now say *amen* without the beginning sound. *(men)*

Say *soon*. Now say *soon* without the beginning sound. *(oon)*

Say *bought*. Now say *bought* without the beginning sound. *(ought)*

Say *noodles*. Now say *noodles* without the beginning sound. *(oodles)*

Working with Clusters

Say *swell*. Now say *swell* with a *m* sound instead of the *w* sound. *(smell)*

Say *tweet*. Now say *tweet* with a *r* sound instead of the *w* sound. *(treat)*

Say *grow*. Now say *grow* with a *l* sound instead of the *r* sound. *(glow)*

Say *blue*. Now say *blue* with a *r* sound instead of the *l* sound. *(brew)*

Say *slim*. Now say *slim* with a *w* sound instead of the *l* sound. *(swim)*

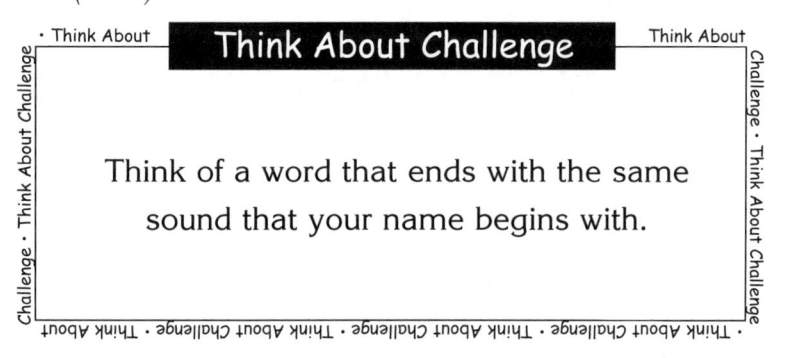

Think About Challenge

Think of a word that ends with the same sound that your name begins with.

Phonological Awareness
Workout #33

☞ When pronouncing an italicized letter (e.g., *t*), be sure to pronounce it by the sound it makes, rather than saying its letter name *(tee)* or adding a vowel to it *(ta)*.

Segmenting Syllables

Tap out the parts (syllables) in the word:
- *magazine* (3)
- *education* (4)
- *cooperation* (5)
- *harmonica* (4)
- *spaghetti* (3)
- *ladybug* (3)

Rhyming

Fill in the blank with a rhyming word.

Pat-a-cake, pat-a-cake, baker's *man*. Bake me a cake as fast as you _____.

Rain, rain, go *away*. Come again some other _____.

Humpty Dumpty sat on a *wall*. Humpty Dumpty had a great _____.

Teddy bear, teddy bear, turn *around*. Teddy bear, teddy bear, touch the _____.

Roses are red. Violets are *blue*. Sugar is sweet, and so are _____.

Blending Sounds

Blend these sounds together. What word do they make?

- *r • ai • n*
- *m • u • ck*
- *b • ee • n*
- *l • oo • k*
- *f • oo • t*
- *z • i • p*

Workout #33

Segmenting Sounds in Words

Does this word end with a *m* sound?

| *pan* (N) | *move* (N) | *wham* (Y) |
| *mouse* (N) | *swim* (Y) | *rim* (Y) |

Manipulating Sounds

Say *boat*. Now say *boat* without the ending sound. *(bow)*

Say *weed*. Now say *weed* without the ending sound. *(wee)*

Say *leap*. Now say *leap* without the ending sound. *(Lee)*

Say *mine*. Now say *mine* without the ending sound. *(my)*

Say *tone*. Now say *tone* without the ending sound. *(toe)*

Working with Clusters

Does this word end with *nt?*

| *wet* (N) | *can't* (Y) | *tune* (N) |
| *went* (Y) | *pant* (Y) | *tint* (Y) |

Think About Challenge

Think of 2 words that almost rhyme, such as *cat* and *hot*. Then tell why they don't rhyme.

Phonological Awareness

Workout #34

> ☞ When pronouncing an italicized letter (e.g., *t*), be sure to pronounce it by the sound it makes, rather than saying its letter name *(tee)* or adding a vowel to it *(ta)*.

Segmenting Syllables

Clap out the parts (syllables) in the word(s):

    ravioli (4)   *emergency* (4)

    potato (3)   *North Carolina* (5)

    rectangle (3)   *November* (3)

Rhyming

Do these two words rhyme?

    tub, hum (N)   *hoop, scoop* (Y)   *merry, bubble* (N)

    ball, tall (Y)   *wire, fire* (Y)   *snap, snip* (N)

Blending Syllables

Blend these parts (syllables) together. What word do they make?

    clock • wise   *con • cert*   *tin • sel*

    fran • tic   *lone • some*   *ad • vance*

Workout #34

Segmenting Sounds in Words

Think of a word that begins with:

th	*j*	*d*
f	*z*	*s*

Manipulating Sounds

Say *I'd*, then say *ride*. What sound makes these two words different? *(r)*

Say *oop*, then say *goop*. What sound makes these two words different? *(g)*

Say *old*, then say *mold*. What sound makes these two words different? *(m)*

Say *Don*, then say *on*. What sound makes these two words different? *(d)*

Say *cup*, then say *up*. What sound makes these two words different? *(c)*

Working with Clusters

Think of a word that begins with:

sk	*gl*	*dr*
sn	*kl*	*sn*

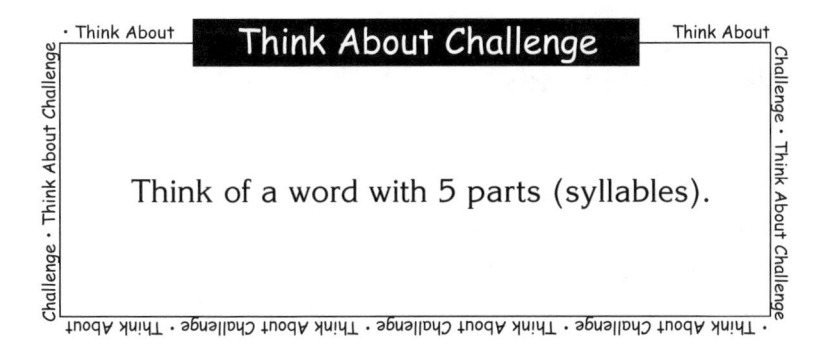

Think About Challenge

Think of a word with 5 parts (syllables).

103

Phonological Awareness
Workout #35

> 👆 When pronouncing an italicized letter (e.g., *t*), be sure to pronounce it by the sound it makes, rather than saying its letter name *(tee)* or adding a vowel to it *(ta)*.

Segmenting Syllables

Give a word that has:
- 3 parts (syllables)
- 4 parts (syllables)
- 5 parts (syllables)

Rhyming

Which of these words rhymes with
- **steal:** *steam, heat,* or **heal?**
- **blubber:** *mother, upper,* or **rubber?**
- **ran:** *pan, rise,* or *rims?*
- **mind:** *lies,* **kind,** or *crib?*
- **sting:** *steam, rang,* or **string?**

Blending Sounds

Does *c* • *oo* • *k* • *ie* say **cookie** or *cooking?*
Does *p* • *o* • *l* • *o* say **polo** or *Pluto?*
Does *l* • *i* • *m* • *a* say *climber* or **lima?**
Does *T* • *i* • *t* • *o* say **Tito** or *teeter?*
Does *sh* • *a* • *ll* • *ow* say *shadow* or **shallow?**

104

Workout #35

Segmenting Sounds in Words

What sound does this word begin with, *v* or *f?*

vote	*funny*	*vine*
vase	*funnel*	*very*

Manipulating Sounds

Say *bug*. Now say *bug* without the beginning sound. *(ugh)*
Say *met*. Now say *met* without the beginning sound. *(et)*
Say *door*. Now say *door* without the beginning sound. *(or)*
Say *leg*. Now say *leg* without the beginning sound. *(egg)*
Say *mat*. Now say *mat* without the beginning sound. *(at)*

Working with Clusters

Say *strap*. Now say *strap* without the beginning sound. *(trap)*
Say *school*. Now say *school* without the beginning sound. *(cool)*
Say *struck*. Now say *struck* without the beginning sound. *(truck)*
Say *shriek*. Now say *shriek* without the beginning sound. *(reek)*
Say *shrine*. Now say *shrine* without the beginning sound. *(Rhine)*

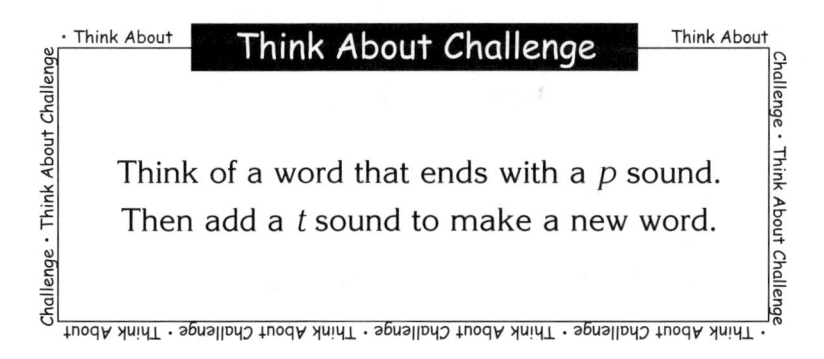

Think About Challenge

Think of a word that ends with a *p* sound.
Then add a *t* sound to make a new word.

Phonological Awareness

Workout #36

☞ When pronouncing an italicized letter (e.g., *t*), be sure to pronounce it by the sound it makes, rather than saying its letter name *(tee)* or adding a vowel to it *(ta)*.

Segmenting Syllables

Are there 3 or 4 parts (syllables) in the word *elevator?* (4)
Are there 4 or 5 parts (syllables) in the word *thermometer?* (4)
Are there 3 or 4 parts (syllables) in the word *furniture?* (3)
Are there 2 or 3 parts (syllables) in the word *sunburn?* (2)
Are there 3 or 4 parts (syllables) in the word *quarterback?* (3)

Rhyming

Give a word that rhymes with:

charge	*broke*	*look*
injure	*peck*	*snicker*

Blending Syllables

Does *two • hun • dred • fif • ty* say **250** or *150?*
Does *ac • ci • den • tal • ly* say **accidentally** or *incidentally?*
Does *straw • ber • ry • Jell • O* say *straw in the bowl* or **strawberry Jell-O?**
Does *civ • i • li • za • tion* say **civilization** or *citation?*
Does *hos • pi • tal • i • ty* say **hospitality** or *hospital?*

106

Workout #36

Segmenting Sounds in Words

Think of a word that ends with the same sound as:

| book | tail | doze |
| ape | beg | sick |

Manipulating Sounds

Say *had*. Now say *had* without the beginning sound. *(add)*
Say *light*. Now say *light* without the ending sound. *(lie)*
Say *bill*. Now say *bill* without the beginning sound. *(ill)*
Say *wide*. Now say *wide* without the ending sound. *(why)*
Say *hit*. Now say *hit* without the beginning sound. *(it)*

Working with Clusters

Does the word have 4 sounds?

| scramble (N) | pants (N) | clean (Y) |
| plant (N) | climb (Y) | grill (Y) |

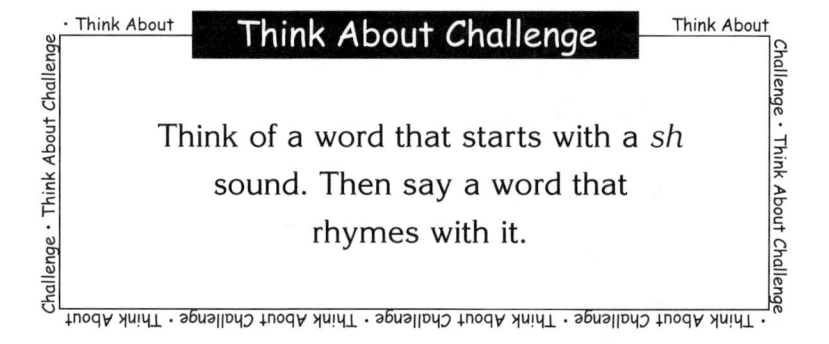

Think About Challenge

Think of a word that starts with a *sh* sound. Then say a word that rhymes with it.

107

Phonological Awareness

Workout #37

> ☞ When pronouncing an italicized letter (e.g., *t*), be sure to pronounce it by the sound it makes, rather than saying its letter name *(tee)* or adding a vowel to it *(ta)*.

Segmenting Syllables

Tell the number of parts (syllables) in the word:

macaroni (4)   *cinnamon* (3)

animal (3)   *hippopotamus* (5)

Alabama (4)   *lawn mower* (3)

Rhyming

Give 2 words that rhyme with:

rose   *stain*   *smell*

room   *stalk*   *motor*

Blending Sounds

Blend these sounds together. What word do they make?

R • o • s • a   *s • o • l • o*   *g • oo • f • y*

m • o • v • ie   *b • o • d • y*   *s • o • f • a*

Workout #37

Segmenting Sounds in Words

What sounds do you hear in this word?

    runner   pitch   then

    bush   reading   sail

Manipulating Sounds

Say *pepper*. Now say *pepper* without the ending sound. *(pep)*

Say *movie*. Now say *movie* without the ending sound. *(move)*

Say *chilly*. Now say *chilly* without the ending sound. *(chill)*

Say *Betty*. Now say *Betty* without the ending sound. *(bet)*

Say *bumpy*. Now say *bumpy* without the ending sound. *(bump)*

Working with Clusters

Blend these sounds together. What word do they make?

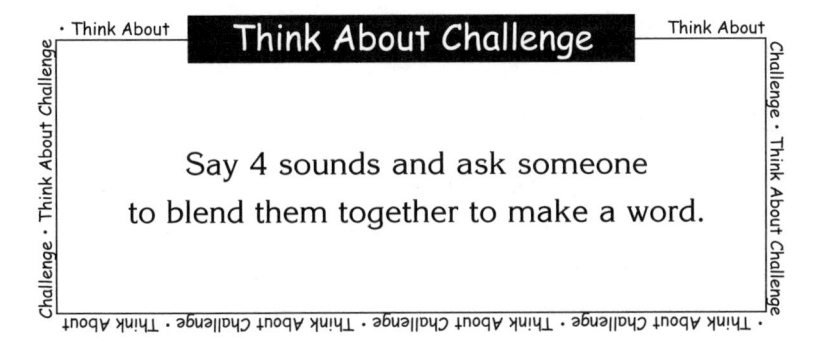

    r • e • s • t   *s • l • i • p*   *d • r • i • p*

    sh • o • pp • ed   *t • r • ea • t*   *l • a • m • p*

Think About Challenge

Say 4 sounds and ask someone to blend them together to make a word.

Phonological Awareness
Workout #38

> ☞ When pronouncing an italicized letter (e.g., *t*), be sure to pronounce it by the sound it makes, rather than saying its letter name *(tee)* or adding a vowel to it *(ta)*.

Segmenting Syllables

Say *toothbrush*. Now say *toothbrush* without *tooth*. *(brush)*
Say *lunchbox*. Now say *lunchbox* without *lunch*. *(box)*
Say *snowstorm*. Now say *snowstorm* without *snow*. *(storm)*
Say *policewoman*. Now say *policewoman* without *woman*. *(police)*
Say *armband*. Now say *armband* without *arm*. *(band)*

Rhyming

Fill in the blank with a rhyming word.
  I before *e* except after _____.
  One, *two*. Buckle my _____.
  Ring around the *rosey*. Pocket full of _____.
  Pete, *Pete*. Stamp your _____.
  Old King *Cole* was a merry old _____.

Blending Syllables

Blend these parts (syllables) together. What word do they make?
  in • fla • ma • tion   def • i • nit • ion
  pre • fer • a • ble   ar • ti • fic • ial
  bi • og • ra • phy   cer • tif • i • cate

Workout #38

Segmenting Sounds in Words

Do these words begin with the same sound?

    thumb, fist (N)   *heat, help* (Y)   *tap, tuna* (Y)

    bunny, point (N)   *sun, super* (Y)   *day, night* (N)

Manipulating Sounds

Say *knee*. Now add a *t* sound to the end of *knee*. *(neat)*

Say *pow*. Now add a *t* sound to the end of *pow*. *(pout)*

Say *row*. Now add a *m* sound to the end of *row*. *(roam)*

Say *too*. Now add a *n* sound to the end of *too*. *(tune)*

Say *doe*. Now add a *z* sound to the end of *doe*. *(doze)*

Working with Clusters

Say *pine*. Now add a *t* sound to the end of *pine*. *(pint)*

Say *for*. Now add a *t* sound to the end of *for*. *(fort)*

Say *close*. Now add a *d* sound to the end of *close*. *(closed)*

Say *top*. Now add a *s* sound to the end of *top*. *(tops)*

Say *pan*. Now add a *z* sound to the end of *pan*. *(pans)*

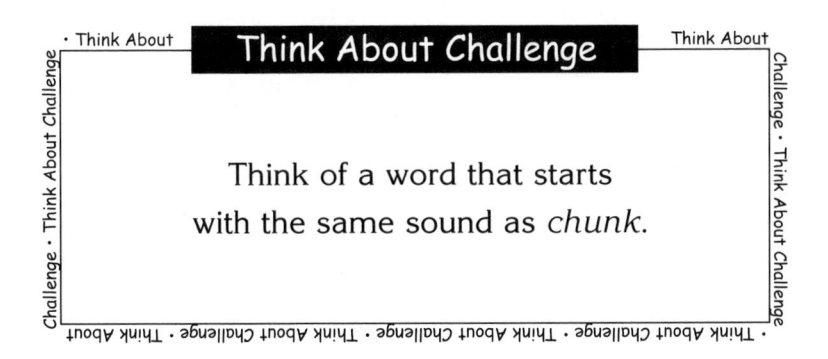

Think About Challenge

Think of a word that starts with the same sound as *chunk*.

Phonological Awareness
Workout #39

> ☞ When pronouncing an italicized letter (e.g., *t*), be sure to pronounce it by the sound it makes, rather than saying its letter name *(tee)* or adding a vowel to it *(ta)*.

Segmenting Syllables

Tap out the parts (syllables) in the word(s):

principal (3)	*vice president* (4)
experiment (4)	*pineapple* (3)
restaurant (3)	*electricity* (5)

Rhyming

Give 2 words that rhyme with:

tipping	*trot*	*pole*
hazy	*queen*	*jive*

Blending Syllables

Does *caf • e • ter • i • a* say *cafeteria?* (Y)

Does *in • ter • me • di • ate* say *intermediate?* (Y)

Does *un • in • te • rrupt • ed* say *uninterested?* (N)

Does *mul • ti • pli • ca • tion* say *duplication?* (N)

Does *a • bbre • vi • a • tion* say *abbreviation?* (Y)

Workout #39

Segmenting Sounds in Words

Does this word have 3 sounds?

lose (Y)	*pine* (Y)	*recess* (N)
at (N)	*may* (N)	*lip* (Y)

Manipulating Sounds

Say *bat*, then say *at*. What sound makes these two words different? *(b)*

Say *cup*, then say *up*. What sound makes these two words different? *(k)*

Say *fin*, then say *in*. What sound makes these two words different? *(f)*

Say *ill*, then say *pill*. What sound makes these two words different? *(p)*

Say *odd*, then say *sod*. What sound makes these two words different? *(s)*

Working with Clusters

What two sounds does this word end with, *pt* or *ps?*

ta**pp**ed *(pt)*	sto**pp**ed *(pt)*	cro**ps**
ta**ps**	sto**ps**	ti**pp**ed *(pt)*

Think About Challenge

Think of 2 small words you could put together to make a bigger word.

113

Phonological Awareness
Workout #40

> ☞ When pronouncing an italicized letter (e.g., *t*), be sure to pronounce it by the sound it makes, rather than saying its letter name *(tee)* or adding a vowel to it *(ta)*.

Segmenting Syllables

Say *flowerpot*. Now say *flowerpot* without *pot*. *(flower)*
Say *butterfly*. Now say *butterfly* without *fly*. *(butter)*
Say *fingerprint*. Now say *fingerprint* without *print*. *(finger)*
Say *popcorn*. Now say *popcorn* without *pop*. *(corn)*
Say *popsicle*. Now say *popsicle* without *sicle*. *(pop)*

Rhyming

Give 3 words that rhyme with:

pug	*sewed*	*crease*
fax	*sight*	*Jan*

Blending Sounds

Does *p • u • pp • ie • s* say **puppies** or *guppies?*
Does *p • e • s • o • s* say *paces* or **pesos?**
Does *c • u • ck • oo • s* say *cruises* or **cuckoos?**
Does *l • e • m • o • n* say **lemon** or *woman?*
Does *v • i • o • l • a* say **viola** or *violet?*

Workout #40

Segmenting Sounds in Words

How many sounds do you hear in the word:

    right (3)   *do* (2)   *sit* (3)

    math (3)   *ship* (3)   *gopher* (4)

Manipulating Sounds

Say *goat*. Now say *goat* without the beginning sound. *(oat)*

Say *apartment*. Now say *apartment* without the beginning sound. *(partment)*

Say *ugly*. Now say *ugly* without the beginning sound. *(glee)*

Say *candy*. Now say *candy* without the beginning sound. *(Andy)*

Say *enough*. Now say *enough* without the beginning sound. *(nough)*

Working with Clusters

Does this word end with *ps?*

    stops (Y)   *tips* (Y)   *store* (N)

    cats (N)   *pops* (Y)   *spine* (N)

Think About Challenge

Say 2 word parts (syllables) very slowly, and ask someone to blend them together to make the word.

Phonological Awareness

Workout #41

> ☞ When pronouncing an italicized letter (e.g., *t*), be sure to pronounce it by the sound it makes, rather than saying its letter name *(tee)* or adding a vowel to it *(ta)*.

Segmenting Syllables

Give a word that has:

    3 parts (syllables)

    4 parts (syllables)

    5 parts (syllables)

Rhyming

Do these two words rhyme?

    frog, hawk (N)   *muffin, puffin* (Y)   *pen, pet* (N)

    bean, beam (N)   *noon, moon* (Y)   *ring, bring* (Y)

Blending Syllables

Does al • pha • be • *tize* say *apologize* or **alphabetize?**

Does ca • tas • tro • *phe* say **catastrophe** or *canopy?*

Does con • cen • tra • *tion* say *complication* or **concentration?**

Does ar • ma • dill • *o* say *amarillo* or **armadillo?**

Does sta • tio • nar • *y* say **stationary** or *station wagon?*

Workout #41

Segmenting Sounds in Words

Do these words end with the same sound?

    leaf, teeth (N)   *wave, wife* (N)   *dad, kid* (Y)
    load, add (Y)   *tell, wall* (Y)   *hat, kit* (Y)

Manipulating Sounds

Say *table*. Now say *table* with a *k* sound instead of the *t* sound. *(cable)*

Say *face*. Now say *face* with a *v* sound instead of the *f* sound. *(vase)*

Say *reaching*. Now say *reaching* with a *t* sound instead of the *r* sound. *(teaching)*

Say *hopper*. Now say *hopper* with a *ch* sound instead of the *h* sound. *(chopper)*

Say *belly*. Now say *belly* with a *j* sound instead of the *b* sound. *(jelly)*

Working with Clusters

What two sounds does this word begin with, *sm* or *sn*?

    *sn*ooze   *sm*oothie   *sm*ile
    *sn*icker   *sn*owman   *sm*ack

Think About Challenge

Think of a word that ends with a vowel sound.

Phonological Awareness
Workout #42

> ☞ When pronouncing an italicized letter (e.g., *t*), be sure to pronounce it by the sound it makes, rather than saying its letter name *(tee)* or adding a vowel to it *(ta)*.

Segmenting Syllables

Tell the number of parts (syllables) in the word(s):

    microwave oven (5)   *ballerina* (4)

    dinosaur (3)   *anniversary* (5)

    operation (4)   *candy bar* (3)

Rhyming

Which word does not rhyme?

    rhyme, **tide,** *time*   *roses,* **blowing,** *noses*

    sound, round, **bounce**   *word, bird,* **hurt**

    scout, *couch, ouch*   *hotel, motel,* **curtain**

Blending Sounds

Blend these sounds together. What word do they make?

    b • i • d   *s • i • gn*   *n • ai • l*

    sh • o • ne   *f • ee • d*   *b • u • n*

Workout #42

Segmenting Sounds in Words

Does this word end with a *s* sound?

| *fuzz* (N) | *because* (N) | *wish* (N) |
| *kiss* (Y) | *mess* (Y) | *sold* (N) |

Manipulating Sounds

Say *off*. Now add a *k* sound to the beginning of *off*. *(cough)*

Say *and*. Now add a *s* sound to the beginning of *and*. *(sand)*

Say *eel*. Now add a *h* sound to the beginning of *eel*. *(heel)*

Say *old*. Now add a *t* sound to the beginning of *old*. *(told)*

Say *ice*. Now add a *v* sound to the beginning of *ice*. *(vice)*

Working with Clusters

What are the sounds in the word:

| *stand* | *trance* | *pans* |
| *pulls* | *trickle* | *ants* |

Think About Challenge

Think of a word to which you could add a sound at the beginning to create a new word.

Phonological Awareness

Workout #43

> When pronouncing an italicized letter (e.g., *t*), be sure to pronounce it by the sound it makes, rather than saying its letter name *(tee)* or adding a vowel to it *(ta)*.

Segmenting Syllables

Say a sentence with:

    3 parts (syllables)

    4 parts (syllables)

    5 parts (syllables)

Rhyming

Give 2 words that rhyme with:

| *wife* | *Mike* | *foam* |
| *eight* | *ant* | *crawling* |

Blending Syllables

Blend these parts (syllables) together. What word do they make?

    fam • i • ly   *un • der • shirt*   *as • tro • naut*

    mol • e • cule   *sill • i • est*   *oc • to • pus*

Workout #43

Segmenting Sounds in Words

What sound does this word begin with, *k* or *g?*

corn (k)   *cone (k)*   *candy (k)*
*g*arage   *g*ummy   *care (k)*

Manipulating Sounds

Say *soak*. Now say *soak* without the ending sound. *(so)*
Say *tomb*. Now say *tomb* without the ending sound. *(to)*
Say *coot*. Now say *coot* without the ending sound. *(coo)*
Say *rove*. Now say *rove* without the ending sound. *(row)*
Say *craze*. Now say *craze* without the ending sound. *(cray)*

Working with Clusters

Say *sweet*. Now say *sweet* with a *l* sound instead of the *w* sound. *(sleet)*

Say *blight*. Now say *blight* with a *r* sound instead of the *l* sound. *(bright)*

Say *graze*. Now say *graze* with a *l* sound instead of the *r* sound. *(glaze)*

Say *slip*. Now say *slip* with a *n* sound instead of the *l* sound. *(snip)*

Say *plod*. Now say *plod* with a *r* sound instead of the *l* sound. *(prod)*

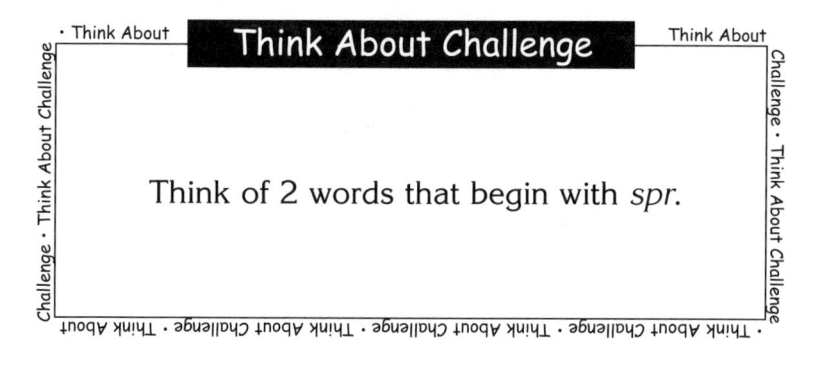

Think About Challenge

Think of 2 words that begin with *spr*.

Phonological Awareness

Workout #44

> ☞ When pronouncing an italicized letter (e.g., *t*), be sure to pronounce it by the sound it makes, rather than saying its letter name *(tee)* or adding a vowel to it *(ta)*.

Segmenting Syllables

Tell the number of parts (syllables) in the word(s):

outer space (3)   *tablespoon* (3)

marshmallows (3)   *population* (4)

South Carolina (5)   *strawberry pie* (4)

Rhyming

Give a word that rhymes with:

sat   *germ*   *broom*

bowling   *cooling*   *beef*

Blending Sounds

Does *m • a • p • le* say **maple** or *Mabel?*

Does *m • o • th • er* say *brother* or **mother?**

Does *s • u • g • ar* say **sugar** or *sucker?*

Does *s • u • pp • er* say *super* or **supper?**

Does *h • a • pp • y* say *sappy* or **happy?**

Workout #44

Segmenting Sounds in Words

Think of a word that begins with:

n	r	sh
j	w	t

Manipulating Sounds

Say *bye*. Now add a *k* sound to the end of *bye*. *(bike)*
Say *way*. Now add a *n* sound to the end of *way*. *(Wayne)*
Say *tea*. Now add a *ch* sound to the end of *tea*. *(teach)*
Say *Kay*. Now add a *t* sound to the end of *Kay*. *(Kate)*
Say *boo*. Now add a *m* sound to the end of *boo*. *(boom)*

Working with Clusters

Say *core*. Now add a *d* sound to the end of *core*. *(cord)*
Say *gone*. Now add a *t* sound to the end of *gone*. *(gaunt)*
Say *coal*. Now add a *d* sound to the end of *coal*. *(cold)*
Say *hun*. Now add a *t* sound to the end of *hun*. *(hunt)*
Say *lass*. Now add a *t* sound to the end of *lass*. *(last)*

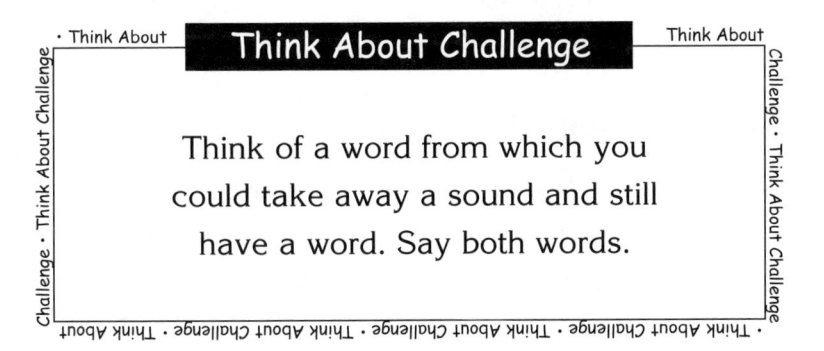

Think About Challenge

Think of a word from which you could take away a sound and still have a word. Say both words.

Phonological Awareness

Workout #45

> ☞ When pronouncing an italicized letter (e.g., *t*), be sure to pronounce it by the sound it makes, rather than saying its letter name *(tee)* or adding a vowel to it *(ta)*.

Segmenting Syllables

Tell how many parts (syllables) are in the whole sentence:
> *Twenty apples are on the tree.* (8)
> *The cat's name is Whiskers.* (6)
> *The bus will be late.* (5)
> *We had brownies for dessert.* (7)
> *The sun is bright.* (4)

Rhyming

Which of these words rhymes with
> ***glove:* love,** *give,* or *move?*
> ***stable:*** *purple,* **Mabel,** or *bubble?*
> ***belt:*** *bell,* **melt,** or *malt?*
> ***kick:*** *like, kite,* or **lick?**
> ***itch:*** *sick,* **stitch,** or *bit?*

Blending Syllables

Blend these parts (syllables) together. What word do they make?
> *ty* • *rann* • *o* • *saur* • *us*   *de* • *ter* • *i* • *o* • *rate*
> *re* • *frig* • *e* • *ra* • *tor*   *a* • *bom* • *in* • *a* • *ble*
> *ge* • *o* • *met* • *ri* • *cal*   *a* • *ppen* • *di* • *ci* • *tis*

Workout #45

Segmenting Sounds in Words

Do you hear a *sh* sound in this word?

soup (N) *pushed* (Y) *sugar* (Y)
service (N) *mushy* (Y) *toss* (N)

Manipulating Sounds

Say *bats,* then say *bat.* What sound was taken away from *bats* to make *bat? (s)*

Say *freeze,* then say *free.* What sound was taken away from *freeze* to make *free? (z)*

Say *fund,* then say *fun.* What sound was taken away from *fund* to make *fun? (d)*

Say *guest,* then say *guess.* What sound was taken away from *guest* to make *guess? (t)*

Say *leaned,* then say *lean.* What sound was taken away from *leaned* to make *lean? (d)*

Working with Clusters

What two sounds does this word begin with, *cl* or *gl?*

clear *glue* *glad*
glory *clap* *clue*

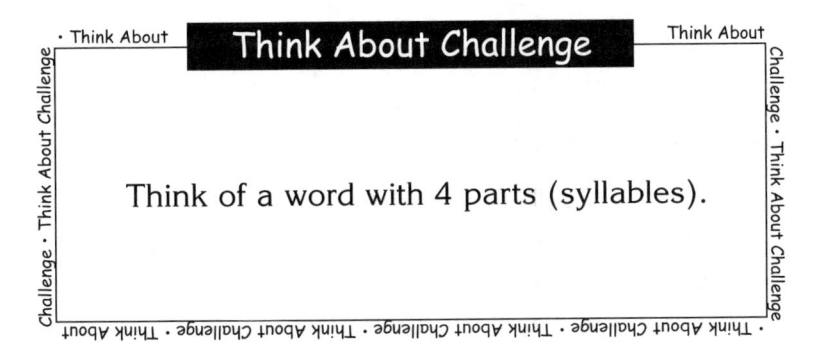

Think About Challenge

Think of a word with 4 parts (syllables).

Phonological Awareness
Workout #46

> 👆 When pronouncing an italicized letter (e.g., *t*), be sure to pronounce it by the sound it makes, rather than saying its letter name *(tee)* or adding a vowel to it *(ta)*.

Segmenting Syllables

Clap out the parts (syllables) in the word:
- *underwater* (4)
- *December* (3)
- *Rollerblading* (4)
- *wonderful* (3)
- *pillowcase* (3)
- *holiday* (3)

Rhyming

Fill in the blank with a rhyming word.

Buy me some peanuts and Cracker*jack*. I don't care if I never get _____.

Diddle, diddle, dumpling, my son *John*. One shoe off and one shoe _____.

He bought me ice cream; he bought me *cake*. He brought me home with a belly _____.

Early to bed. Early to *rise*. Makes a person healthy, wealthy, and _____.

Jack be nimble. Jack be *quick*. Jack jump over the candle _____.

Blending Syllables

Does *con • ver • sa • tion* say complication or **conversation?**
Does *wa • ter • mel • on* say **watermelon** or waterfall?
Does *ther • mom • e • ter* say barometer or **thermometer?**
Does *res • pi • ra • tion* say **respiration** or perspiration?
Does *pres • er • va • tion* say reservation or **preservation?**

Workout #46

Segmenting Sounds in Words

Does this word begin with a *p* sound?

    taxi (N)   *perfect* (Y)   *pickle* (Y)

    binder (N)   *mop* (N)   *paper* (Y)

Manipulating Sounds

Say *mash*. Now say *mash* without the beginning sound. *(ash)*

Say *lion*. Now say *lion* without the beginning sound. *(ion)*

Say *coffee*. Now say *coffee* without the beginning sound. *(offee)*

Say *tiptoe*. Now say *tiptoe* without the beginning sound. *(iptoe)*

Say *table*. Now say *table* without the beginning sound. *(able)*

Working with Clusters

Think of a word that begins with the same two sounds as:

    print   *clap*   *snoop*

    trick   *spoon*   *skunk*

Think About Challenge

Think of a word that ends with the same sound as *lounge*.

Phonological Awareness

Workout #47

> ☞ When pronouncing an italicized letter (e.g., *t*), be sure to pronounce it by the sound it makes, rather than saying its letter name *(tee)* or adding a vowel to it *(ta)*.

Segmenting Syllables

Say *skyscraper*. Now say *skyscraper* without *scraper*. *(sky)*

Say *windowsill*. Now say *windowsill* without *sill*. *(window)*

Say *bookmark*. Now say *bookmark* without *book*. *(mark)*

Say *turtleneck*. Now say *turtleneck* without *turtle*. *(neck)*

Say *copycat*. Now say *copycat* without *copy*. *(cat)*

Rhyming

Do these two words rhyme?

    bolt, colt (Y)   *deck, dock* (N)

    thistle, whistle (Y)   *leather, weather* (Y)

    bag, big (N)   *cry, try* (Y)

Blending Syllables

Blend these sounds together. What word do they make?

    c • a • n • o • py   *l • o • c • a • te*   *b • a • b • ie • s*

    r • e • s • i • de   *c • o • p • i • er*   *p • i • t • a • s*

Workout #47

Segmenting Sounds in Words

Think of a word that ends with:

| k | ch | f |
| d | s | t |

Manipulating Sounds

Say *hă*. Now add a *t* sound to the end of *hă*. *(hat)*
Say *că*. Now add a *b* sound to the end of *că*. *(cab)*
Say *sigh*. Now add a *t* sound to the end of *sigh*. *(sight)*
Say *toe*. Now add a *d* sound to the end of *toe*. *(toad)*
Say *Bo*. Now add a *n* sound to the end of *Bo*. *(bone)*

Working with Clusters

Say *hand*. Now say *hand* without the *n* sound. *(had)*
Say *lisp*. Now say *lisp* without the *s* sound. *(lip)*
Say *quilt*. Now say *quilt* without the *l* sound. *(quit)*
Say *moons*. Now say *moons* without the *n* sound. *(moos)*
Say *chomp*. Now say *chomp* without the *m* sound. *(chop)*

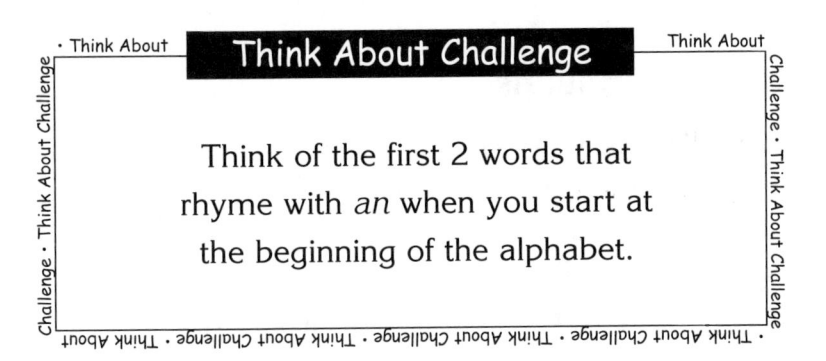

Think About Challenge

Think of the first 2 words that rhyme with *an* when you start at the beginning of the alphabet.

Phonological Awareness

Workout #48

> ☞ When pronouncing an italicized letter (e.g., *t*), be sure to pronounce it by the sound it makes, rather than saying its letter name *(tee)* or adding a vowel to it *(ta)*.

Segmenting Syllables

Give a person's name that has:
- 3 parts (syllables)
- 4 parts (syllables)
- 5 parts (syllables)

Rhyming

Which of these words rhymes with
- *volley:* hill, **holly,** or starry?
- *dock:* **flock,** hook, or duck?
- *jingle:* **mingle,** jungle, or jangle?
- *lung:* lose, **stung,** or song?
- *spinner:* banner, **thinner,** or spun?

Blending Sounds

Does *l • o • ck • e • t* say rocket or **locket?**

Does *ll • a • m • a • s* say **llamas** or pajamas?

Does *m • o • v • i • ng* say **moving** or movie?

Does *r • ai • n • b • ow* say raindrop or **rainbow?**

Does *g • ue • ss • i • ng* say **guessing** or pressing?

Workout #48

Segmenting Sounds in Words

Think of a word that begins with the same sound as:

| pig | hope | kind |
| pine | mom | ten |

Manipulating Sounds

Say *fiddle*. Now say *fiddle* with a ă sound rather than the ĭ sound. *(faddle)*

Say *tiny*. Now say *tiny* with a ō sound rather than the ī sound. *(Tony)*

Say *smiley*. Now say *smiley* with a ĕ sound rather than the ī sound. *(smelly)*

Say *raffle*. Now say *raffle* with a ŭ sound rather than the ă sound. *(ruffle)*

Say *kettle*. Now say *kettle* with a ă sound rather than the ĕ sound. *(cattle)*

Working with Clusters

Blend these sounds together. What word do they make?

m • oo • n • l • igh • t   ch • i • l • d • r • e • n

s • t • u • d • e • n • t   th • i • n • k • i • ng

p • r • o • g • r • a • m   p • l • a • nn • i • ng

Think About Challenge

Think of a word that ends with the same sound the word *thanks* begins with.

Phonological Awareness

Workout #49

☞ When pronouncing an italicized letter (e.g., *t*), be sure to pronounce it by the sound it makes, rather than saying its letter name *(tee)* or adding a vowel to it *(ta)*.

Segmenting Syllables

Say a sentence with:

    5 parts (syllables)

    6 parts (syllables)

    7 parts (syllables)

Rhyming

Give 2 words that rhyme with:

quail	*badly*	*things*
call	*roar*	*zinc*

Blending Sounds

Blend these sounds together. What word do they make?

p • o • g • o	*d • i • tt • o*	*m • e • ss • y*
m • a • n • y	*m • a • m • a*	*e • m • ai • l*

Segmenting Sounds in Words

What sound does this word end with, *m* or *n*?

| *rhyme* | *ran* | *trim* |
| *win* | *whine* | *some* |

Manipulating Sounds

Say *gravy*, then say *grave*. What sound was taken away from *gravy* to make *grave*? (ē)

Say *yellow*, then say *yell*. What sound was taken away from *yellow* to make *yell*? (ō)

Say *jelly*, then say *jell*. What sound was taken away from *jelly* to make *jell*? (ē)

Say *bellow*, then say *bell*. What sound was taken away from *bellow* to make *bell*? (ō)

Say *July*, then say *Jul*. What sound was taken away from *July* to make *Jul*? (ī)

Working with Clusters

Does this word begin with *br*?

| *brick* (Y) | *price* (N) | *bright* (Y) |
| *bring* (Y) | *board* (N) | *broom* (Y) |

Think About Challenge

Think of a word with 1 part (syllable). Then add a sound to make a new word. Say both words.

Phonological Awareness

Workout #50

> ☞ When pronouncing an italicized letter (e.g., *t*), be sure to pronounce it by the sound it makes, rather than saying its letter name *(tee)* or adding a vowel to it *(ta)*.

Segmenting Syllables

Tap out the parts (syllables) in the word(s):

auditorium (5)   *porcupine* (3)

triangle (3)   *peanut butter* (4)

apologize (4)   *computer* (3)

Rhyming

Which word does not rhyme?

river, **quicken,** *quiver*   *any,* **money,** *many*

mini, *city, kitty*   *silk,* **salt,** *milk*

things, wings, **songs**   *side,* **sight,** *tide*

Blending Syllables

Blend these parts (syllables) together. What word do they make?

doc • tor   is • land   shoe • lace

sun • set   re • spect   dir • ty

Workout #50

Segmenting Sounds in Words

Think of a word that ends with the same sound as:

    bib   *save*   *tape*

    swan   *duck*   *puffy*

Manipulating Sounds

Say *cow*. Now add a *ch* sound to the end of *cow*. *(couch)*

Say *inch*. Now add a *p* sound to the beginning of *inch*. *(pinch)*

Say *edge*. Now add a *h* sound to the beginning of *edge*. *(hedge)*

Say *toe*. Now add a *t* sound to the end of *toe*. *(tote)*

Say *die*. Now add a *m* sound to the end of *die*. *(dime)*

Working with Clusters

Blend these sounds together. What word do they make?

    s • p • ee • d • i • ng   *h • a • m • b • ur • g • er*

    s • a • n • d • w • i • ch   *m • ou • n • t • ai • n*

    g • l • a • ss • e • s   *c • r • u • n • ch • e • s*

Think About Challenge

Say 3 word parts (syllables) very slowly and ask someone to blend them together to make a word.

Notes:

Notes: